World War II

UPDATED EDITION

MAURICE ISSERMAN

JOHN S. BOWMAN
GENERAL EDITOR

Facts On File, Inc.

Note on Photos
Many of the illustrations and photographs used in this book are old,
historical images. The quality of the prints is not always up to modern
standards, as in some cases the originals are from glass negatives or are damaged.
The content of the illustrations, however, made their inclusion important
despite problems in reproduction.

World War II, Updated Edition
Copyright © 2003, 1991 by Maurice Isserman
Maps copyright © 2003 by Facts On File

All rights reserved. No part of this book may be reproduced or utilized in any form
or by any means, electronic or mechanical, including photocopying, recording, or by
any information storage or retrieval systems, without permission in writing from the
publisher. For information contact:

Facts On File, Inc.
132 West 31st Street
New York NY 10001

Library of Congress Cataloging-in-Publication Data
Isserman, Maurice
World War II / by Maurice Isserman.—Updated ed.
p. cm.—(America at War)
Includes bibliographical references and index.
ISBN 0-8160-4938-6
1. World War, 1939–1945—United States. 2. United States—History—
1933–1945. I. Title: World War 2. II. Title: World War Two. III. Title. IV. Series.
D769 .I87 2003
940.53—dc21   2002005504

Facts On File books are available at special discounts when purchased in bulk quantities for businesses, associations, institutions, or sales promotions. Please call our
Special Sales Department in New York at (212) 967-8800 or (800) 322-8755.

You can find Facts On File on the World Wide Web at http://www.factsonfile.com

Text design by Erika K. Arroyo
Logo design by Smart Graphics
Maps by Jeremy Eagle

Printed in the United States of America

MP FOF 10 9 8 7 6 5 4 3 2

This book is printed on acid-free paper.

Contents

Preface

World War II was the greatest and most costly conflict in the history of humanity. It redrew the political map of Europe and Asia. It transformed the United States and its wartime ally the Soviet Union into superpowers and laid the groundwork for the conflicts of the cold war that would shape international affairs for the next four and a half decades. Like all major wars, its impact reached far beyond the realm of its military and diplomatic outcome, for it set in motion far-reaching social, cultural, and political changes. World War II is, without question and deservedly, the most closely studied event of the 20th century.

That is not to say, however, that there is any consensus as to how the war should be regarded these many years later. For many Americans it is and has always been the "Good War"—a high and holy cause whose righteousness was enshrined in the shining victory of 1945. Gen. Dwight D. Eisenhower, commander of Allied military forces in the European theater of the war, would entitle his 1948 memoir of the war years *Crusade in Europe.* Others, including some veterans of the war, are more skeptical. Paul Fussell, a young American second lieutenant commanding a rifle platoon in France who was severely wounded in combat in the spring of 1945, concluded in his 1989 book *Wartime: Understanding and Behavior in the Second World War,* that no war could ever be judged a "good" war if one takes into account the full measure of pain and suffering it has produced. America, he wrote, "has not yet truly understood what the Second World War was like."

Whether or not they have arrived at a full understanding of the war's meaning, Americans certainly cannot be accused of having ignored the war in recent years. If anything, the farther the war has receded into the past, the greater the interest seems to have grown. In the years since this volume was first published in 1991, books about the war have crowded newspaper best-seller lists, websites devoted to the conflict have proliferated on the Internet, and movies about D day and Pearl Harbor have packed audiences into cineplexes. A museum devoted to the D day invasion opened in New Orleans, Louisiana, and tens of thousands of American tourists traveled to Normandy, France, to see the actual invasion beaches and to walk among the rows of crosses in the U.S. military cemetery on the grassy bluff overlooking Omaha Beach. As for cable TV's History Channel, as one historian noted, it seemed "to live on Second World War film shot by U.S. Army Signal Corps combat photographers."

Attention to the history of the war in the 1990s was inspired in part by the 50th anniversary observances that rolled along at regular intervals between 1991 and 1995. But the remembrances themselves were also tinged with the bittersweet knowledge that the World War II generation was itself fast disappearing from the scene, and with its demise the chances for the children and grandchildren of the veterans to express their gratitude would soon be over as well. By 1999 there were only about 5 million American veterans of World War II still alive, one-third of the 15 million men and women who had served in the U.S. armed forces between 1941 and 1945. These World War II veterans, now men and women in their seventies, eighties, and nineties, were reportedly dying off at a rate of more than 1,100 every day, which meant that their annual mortality from natural causes was greater than the total U.S. combat deaths during the entire period of the war. Citing the need to act before the last of the participants were no longer alive to appreciate the gesture, Congress authorized the construction of the National World War II Memorial in Washington, D.C., at a location on the Mall between the Lincoln Memorial and the Washington Monument, the only 20th-century event to be commemorated on the Mall's central axis.

As the 20th century drew to an end, many Americans who had not been alive at the time of the war clearly found its memory a source of patriotic and personal inspiration. General Eisenhower's characterization of the war as a crusade seemed entirely apt to them. The wartime years, at least in retrospect, seemed to represent an era when moral and political choices were simpler and more satisfying than those offered to succeeding generations. The United States had gone to war in 1941 for the clearest of reasons: Its armed forces and national security were under attack from foreign enemies. There was no ambiguity about the nature of America's foes in the war, who had clearly demonstrated that they represented forces of evil and aggression through both their beliefs and their actions. The story of the war followed an easily understandable and very satisfying narrative line; after initial setbacks, the Allies mustered the resources and resolve to go on the offensive, and from late 1942 through the spring and summer of 1945 launched ever more devastating attacks on the Axis powers.

The world was certainly left a better place for the defeat of Nazi Germany and imperial Japan in 1945 at the hands of the United States and its wartime allies. World War II also left the United States a superpower, possessor of the most powerful industrial base and military machine in human history. And if, as noted, the events of 1941–45 ushered in a new and even more protracted international conflict, the cold war between the United States and its former ally and new rival, the Soviet Union, it also left Americans with the confidence that they would ultimately prevail over this enemy, just as they had over the Germans and the Japanese in the earlier war.

The veterans themselves, in the eyes of their children and grandchildren, had come over the years to embody the virtues of the cause they had served. The "greatest generation," as NBC news anchor Tom Brokaw called World War II veterans in his best-selling book of that title, had gone to war reluctantly, but they had sacrificed themselves unstintingly. These were quintessentially American "citizen soldiers," as historian Stephen Ambrose referred to them in the title of another best-selling book about the war, who proved that democratic values could prevail over tyranny and terror. In the 1998 Steven Spielberg epic *Saving Private Ryan,* actor Tom Hanks ably represented the greatest generation/citizen soldier. Hanks's character, an infantry captain who landed with his men in the first wave on Omaha Beach on June 6, 1944, was described as a schoolteacher in civilian life, an ordinary man whose hands shook as he tried to drink from a canteen as his landing craft approached the beach. And yet, faced with the full horror of war (as represented by some truly spectacular special effects in the opening minutes of the movie), he proved himself a brave and able warrior. In the end, at the cost of his own life, he fulfilled his mission, stemmed the German counterattack, and saved young Private Ryan to go home to his family and his country. It was a simple tale, powerfully told, and certainly captured a central aspect of the war's meaning for Americans.

The celebration of the heroism of the "greatest generation" became so commonplace in the 1990s that by the start of the new century it became a topic for some affectionately humorous commentary in American comic pages. In a strip that ran in the nation's newspapers in the late summer of 2001, "Doonesbury" creator Garry Trudeau had one of his baby-boom-generation characters, radio host Mark Slackmeyer, visit his ailing World War II veteran father in the hospital. "Dad, when I heard about your latest close call," a concerned-looking Mark declared at his father's bedside, "I started thinking about all the things I don't really know about you. . . . Especially all the remarkable challenges you and your generation faced during the war." To which his unimpressed father responds wearily, "Great. Another [baby] boomer with hedgerow envy." "No, no," Mark hastily says, "This isn't a Spielberg thing."

Trudeau might just as well have had Mark say "This isn't an Ambrose thing," because Stephen Ambrose's books on the war also carried a distinct whiff of "hedgerow envy," even as they made Ambrose a best-selling author. The popularity of books like his *D-Day* and *Citizen Soldiers*, with sales in hardcover and paperback running into hundreds of thousands of copies (not to mention such commercial spin-offs as the Stephen Ambrose World War II calendar) had a lot to do with his determined and unwavering celebration of American virtue in the war. As Ambrose wrote in his 1991 book, *Band of Brothers* (later made into an HBO series that ran in fall 2001, produced by Steven Spielberg and Tom Hanks):

> The Americans established a moral superiority over the Germans . . . based on better training methods, better selection methods for command positions, ultimately on a more open army reflecting a more open society. Democracy proved better able to produce young men who could be made into superb soldiers than Nazi Germany.

As a historical explanation for the victory of the United States in World War II, this clearly was intended to appeal to the average American reader; after all, who would not feel pleased to be living in a country where Might and Right were depicted as being so closely linked? But Ambrose's style of argument raised troublesome questions in the minds of other historians. For one thing, the Germans and Japanese produced some pretty good soldiers themselves in World War II, and in the early years of that conflict won victory after victory over their democratic opponents. Moreover, the Red Army of the Soviet Union played no small role in the final defeat of Nazi Germany, even though Soviet soldiers were hardly the products of any kind of "open society." A good storyteller, Ambrose was not perhaps the most reliable interpreter of the ultimate meaning of the stories he recounted—prone to the display of a little too much "hedgerow envy," and not always enough critical distance.

America's role in World War II found a less celebratory treatment in the works of other professional historians writing at the end of the 20th century. America's "fervent defense of freedom," Professor Ronald Takaki of the University of California, Berkeley wrote in his *Double Victory: A Multicultural History of America in World War II*, published in 2000, "was accompanied by a hypocritical disregard for our nation's declaration that 'all men are created equal.'"

> The war against Nazi Germany was fought with a jim crow [racially segregated] army. During the fight against Hitler's ideology of Aryan supremacy, ethnic enmities exploded in race riots in cities like Los Angeles and Detroit. The President who led the fight for freedom also signed Executive Order 9066 for the evacuation and internment of 120,000 Japanese Americans without due process of law.

If the war was capable of bringing out the best in the men who were sent to fight in it, it could also show up some of the defects of a society at home—even an open society like that of the United States—as it devoted itself to the pursuit of military victory abroad. Professor David Kennedy of the Stanford University history department offered another reading of the war that was darker than anything to be found in Ambrose's works, in the conclusion to his Pulitzer prize–winning 1999 book, *Freedom from Fear: The American People in Depression and War, 1929–1945*. According to Kennedy:

> Americans could not see [the] future clearly in 1945, but they could look back over the war they had just waged. They might have reflected with some discomfort on how slowly they had awakened to the menace of Hitlerism in the isolationist 1930s; on how callously they had barred the door to those seeking to flee from Hitler's Europe; on how

heedlessly they had provoked Japan into a probably avoidable war in a region where few American interests were at stake; on how they had largely fought with America's money and machines and with Russia's men.

And he went on in that vein for several more paragraphs. The newspaper columnist George Will was so outraged by Kennedy's failure to hew to Stephen Ambrose's upbeat approach to the war's history, that he called on Stanford University students to boycott Kennedy's classes—without noticeable effect.

A more reasonable criticism of Takaki and Kennedy's depressing account of wartime hypocrisy and duplicity is that the war itself contributed to the emergence of new and more powerful movements for equal rights in the United States after the war. Having gone to war for the "Four Freedoms" abroad, hundreds of thousands of African-American veterans (as well as members of other racial minorities) were not about to settle for less at home.

There was an even greater controversy when the historical curators at the Smithsonian Air and Space Museum in Washington, D.C., considered mounting an exhibition commemorating the 50th anniversary of the bombing of Hiroshima in a way that, to outraged veterans' groups, seemed to imply that the United States owed Japan an apology for dropping the bomb. Congress quickly got into the act, condemning the offending historians and threatening federal appropriations for the Smithsonian. The result was that, in the end, the exhibition was simply canceled; the public was the loser. The proper way to remember the "Good War"—a period nostalgically celebrated for its supposed national unity—had thus, ironically, become something over which Americans fought among themselves some 50 years later.

This volume on World War II in the America at War series will not resolve the controversies over how Americans should remember the events of 1941–45. As a history of American involvement in the war it is occasionally critical, where criticism seems justified and unavoidable. But it is at the same time written in a spirit respectful of both the American cause in the war and the men and women who wore their country's uniform in its defense. The intent of this book is not to offer final and irrefutable answers to difficult historical questions, such as whether or not the United States should have dropped atomic bombs on Hiroshima and Nagasaki in August 1945, but rather to serve as a general introduction for students and others beginning to think about the history of the war and its many legacies, for better or for worse.

To this end, this revised edition offers many new features. In addition to an expanded collection of photographs and maps, and an updated and expanded bibliography at the end of the text, the reader will also find short box features spaced throughout the narrative, discussing topics ranging from the experience of American prisoners of war at the hands of the Germans and Japanese, to the military and symbolic importance of the jeep to the war effort, to an appreciation of the combat record of African-American aviators. Readers will also find a glossary at the end of the book, providing a quick reference to understand some of the more obscure and difficult terms that appear in the text.

Were the generation of Americans who fought in World War II, and who are now passing from the scene, the "greatest generation"? The title was not one that the World War II generation chose for itself, and many of them felt uncomfortable when it was applied to them. What can be said, without exaggeration, is that this was a generation greatly tested in its youth by circumstances not of its making, forced into facing up to the kind of challenge that no generation would freely choose for itself. Hopefully the pages that follow will illustrate why such a claim alone should be considered honor enough for any generation while at the same time they invite the reader to examine the war in the larger context of important historical issues.

1

SPLITTING
THE WORLD

Leo Szilard was a worried man in 1939. A Hungarian-born physicist and electrical engineer, Szilard had recently moved to the United States. For several years he had been among a small group of scientists around the world who were investigating ways to tap the tremendous potential for energy locked up within the atom. If the nucleus, or innermost part, of certain atoms could be split, the result would be "nuclear fission." The possibilities were staggering. Split enough atoms in a controlled nuclear reaction, Szilard reasoned, and you could provide enough power to light up a city—or destroy one.

In the spring of this last year of the 1930s it seemed as though several European scientists were about to realize Szilard's dream. Why, then, was Szilard terrified by the prospect of success? Because the scientists who had made the most progress in nuclear fission worked for the Kaiser Wilhelm Institute in Berlin, Germany. The fruits of their research were going to benefit the Nazi government ruled by Adolf Hitler.

Szilard was very familiar with the Kaiser Wilhelm Institute because he had worked in one of its branches himself in the 1920s after completing his studies in physics at the University of Berlin. Szilard would have been happy to remain in Germany, pursuing his research. Instead there were dramatic changes in that country's political life in the 1930s, and Szilard, who was Jewish, was forced to flee the country after Hitler took over in 1933.

Many Germans had felt humiliated by their defeat in the world war of 1914–18. After suffering through postwar economic hardships and the worldwide depression of the 1930s, they were looking for scapegoats. Hitler was able to channel the Germans' frustration into support for his extreme doctrines of anti-Semitism, or hatred of Jews. The Nazis blamed most of Germany's problems on the Jews, and made it clear from their first days in power that there was no place for them in the "Third Reich," Hitler's name for the new German empire he proposed to build. As a refugee Szilard moved first to England, where he raised money to help other scientists escape from Germany. Then, in 1938, he sailed to the United States and settled in New York.

That year proved to be the last full year of peace that the world would know for a long time. It was a peace bought at a heavy price. Szilard followed the news that year with mounting fear that Europe was once again heading toward war. In September 1938 British prime minister Neville Chamberlain and French premier Eduard Daladier had met with Hitler in Munich in a desperate effort to prevent the outbreak of war. Having greatly expanded Germany's military establishment since coming to power, Hitler was growing ever more ambitious in his plans for expanding Germany's size and power. His troops had already marched into Austria earlier in 1938. Now he demanded that Czechoslovakia, which had a sizable German-speaking minority living within its borders, hand over a large chunk of its territory known as the Sudetenland to Germany.

Chamberlain believed that Hitler's ambitions could be appeased and war averted by giving this territory to Germany. And so, without consulting the Czechs, he agreed to the "Munich Pact." In return for Hitler's assurance that he would respect the independence of the remaining portion of

Adolf Hitler came to power in 1933. *(Library of Congress)*

Hitler leads his storm troopers in Nazi salute. Jackbooted Mussolini stands respectfully in foreground. *(Library of Congress)*

Czechoslovakia, Chamberlain agreed that the Sudetenland should be handed over. Czechoslovakia, which could not defend itself without British and French assistance, had no choice but to give in.

Many people were relieved that Chamberlain had been able to secure a promise of what he called "peace in our time" from Hitler. But others, like Szilard, remained worried that Hitler would not be satisfied with the Sudetenland. They believed that sooner or later the Western democracies were going to have to make a stand against him. If the world was headed for another war, it was absolutely essential that Hitler's enemies, not Hitler's scientists, be the first to unlock the secrets of nuclear fission.

Short, chubby, intense, and bespectacled, speaking English with a thick Hungarian accent, Szilard knew as much as anyone about the inner workings of the atom. But Szilard did not have a clue as to how to get things done in his newly adopted homeland. Most of his close friends and associates in the United States were also refugees and were equally lost in the world of practical affairs. One of those who shared Szilard's worries was Enrico Fermi, a Nobel Prize–winning Italian physicist, who had fled to the United States in January 1939. Fermi's wife was Jewish, and he had feared for her safety, when the Fascist dictator of Italy, Benito Mussolini, began to copy the anti-Semitic measures of his ally Hitler.

Fermi, Szilard, and other refugee scientists met in New York that spring of 1939 to discuss the new developments in nuclear physics and their possible applications. They decided they had to let someone in the American government know about these possibilities but were not sure whom to go to. Since there was no U.S. government agency that monitored scientific developments, they decided that perhaps one of the military services would be interested.

To find out, Fermi paid his own way down to Washington, D.C., in March 1939, the month that Hitler broke his Munich promise by taking over the rest of Czechoslovakia. Fermi set up a meeting with officials

Enrico Fermi, Italian-American physicist, received the 1938 Nobel Prize in physics for identifying new elements and discovering nuclear reactions by his method of nuclear irradiation and bombardment.
(National Archives)

from the U.S. Navy and tried in his heavily accented English to explain to them the basic principles of nuclear physics. The navy's representatives were unimpressed. Was any of this going to be of any practical use to them in the near future, say as a source of energy to propel submarines, or as a weapon of war? Fermi could not say for sure. The navy officials regarded him as an impractical dreamer. Szilard made another attempt later that spring to interest the navy in his experiments, with as little success as Fermi.

While Szilard's circle of refugee scientists continued to worry over their inability to interest anyone in their ideas, the months of peace left to the world were rapidly decreasing in number. After finishing off Czechoslovakia, Hitler turned his attention to Poland, with a new series of territorial demands. But Britain and France were finally growing disillusioned with the "appeasement" policies they had pursued until then. They promised the Polish government to come to its aid in the event of a German attack. The American president, Franklin Roosevelt, condemned the German occupation of Czechoslovakia and offered to mediate the growing disputes in Europe in an international conference. Hitler and Mussolini contemptuously rejected the offer.

In July of 1939 Szilard had another idea. The American government did not appear to be interested in exploring the potential of nuclear fission. Perhaps he could at least hinder the Nazi scientists by limiting their access to uranium, the radioactive element that was proving most useful in experiments. One of the world's main sources of uranium was to be found in Belgium's African colony, the Belgian Congo. Along with Eugene Wigner, another refugee physicist, Szilard decided to send a message to the Belgian government to warn it of the dangers of selling uranium to the Germans. The man to contact the Belgians, they decided, was another refugee from Nazi oppression, one of Szilard's old teachers from the University of Berlin, Albert Einstein.

The German-born Einstein had been living in Princeton, New Jersey, since 1933. Like Szilard, Einstein was Jewish. Because of that, and his pronounced anti-Nazi sentiments, the Nazis had seized his property and stripped him of German citizenship. (He would become an American citizen in 1940.) Einstein was probably the most celebrated scientist of his era. He was known for his theoretical work in physics, and especially for the formula $e = mc^2$: Energy equals mass times the speed of light squared. What this meant in simple terms was that there was

Professor Albert Einstein *(Library of Congress)*

an enormous amount of energy stored within the atomic structure of matter. But Einstein was not yet convinced that there was any practical way of releasing that energy, and he had not kept up with the most recent developments in the study of nuclear physics.

That did not make any difference to Szilard and Wigner. What they needed was a name that would command attention, and Einstein's name could do that. On a hot day in mid-July 1939 they drove out to the village on Long Island, New York, where Einstein was spending the summer. The distinguished white-haired physicist met them at his cottage door wearing a T-shirt and a pair of rolled-up pants. Despite the informality of the setting, it proved a momentous meeting.

Einstein quickly grasped both the scientific and political importance of what Szilard and Wigner had to tell him. A lifelong pacifist, he did not like the idea of helping any government develop a terrible new military weapon. However, Einstein was gravely troubled by the prospect of a Nazi atomic bomb and agreed to act as intermediary with the Belgian government. He dictated a letter in German to the Belgian ambassador, which Wigner and Szilard took away with them to translate and revise. The three men also agreed that, if they were to contact a foreign government, they should advise the U.S. State Department of their plans. But that decision confronted Szilard with the problem he had already faced: How did one go about informing the American government about such complex matters?

The solution was offered by a man named Alexander Sachs, whom Szilard contacted through a mutual friend. Sachs, an economist and vice president of a New York financial firm, had worked for Franklin Roosevelt's administration for three years in the early 1930s. He remained on friendly terms with the president. When Sachs met with Szilard, he convinced him that Einstein's letter should go directly to Roosevelt. Sachs volunteered to carry it to the White House and deliver it personally into the president's hands to make sure it got the attention it deserved. Over the next few weeks Szilard reworked the letter in consultation with Einstein, and on August 15, 1939, he delivered a final draft to Sachs.

"It may be possible," Einstein's letter informed the president, "to set up nuclear chain reactions in a large mass of uranium, by which vast amounts of power and large quantities of new radium-like elements would be generated." If so, the letter went on to warn, in cautiously worded phrases, "it is conceivable—though much less certain—that extremely powerful bombs of a new type may thus be constructed." Such a bomb might prove too heavy to deliver in an aerial attack, but if smuggled into a port aboard ship it "might very well destroy the whole port together with some of the surrounding territory."

WORLD WAR II

While Szilard, Einstein, and their associates worried about weapons as yet unproven and unbuilt, the Nazis unleashed a mass slaughter with the more conventional weapons already at their command. On September 1, 1939, the *Wehrmacht* (the German army) and the *Luftwaffe* (the German air force) began an unprovoked assault on Poland. The Poles, vastly outnumbered and underequipped, fought bravely but were defeated before the month ended. England and France declared war on Germany on September 3, and the Second World War had officially begun.

In his Princeton study, Einstein discussed the role of science in the Allies' war effort with (seated) Capt. Geoffrey E. Sage, commanding officer of the U.S. Naval Training School at Princeton, and Lt. Comdr. Frederick L. Douthit, USNR, executive officer of the school. *(Library of Congress)*

2

BACKGROUND
TO WAR

When the Second World War began in September 1939, less than 21 years had passed since the end of the First World War. The war of 1914–18 had pitted Germany and the Austro-Hungarian empire against England, France, Russia, Italy (from May 1915), and the United States (from April 1917). It had cost the lives of more than 10,000,000 soldiers and civilians. It had also turned the old political order upside down in Europe. By the end of the war, the Russian czar, the German kaiser, and the Austro-Hungarian emperor had all been overthrown by their own peoples. Newly independent nations, including Finland, Poland, Czechoslovakia, and Yugoslavia, were carved from the wreckage of the czarist Russian and Austro-Hungarian Empires. Many in Europe were able to vote in free elections and enjoy other democratic freedoms for the first time.

But the politicians, diplomats, and generals who had presided over the so-called war to end all wars also bequeathed a legacy of political extremism, economic hardship, and nationalist resentments that would trouble and in the end obliterate the fragile postwar peace. In 1917 war weariness in Russia led to demonstrations and riots by soldiers and civilians, culminating in the seizure of power by the Bolshevik (later known as the Communist) Party and the founding of the Soviet Union. Soviet communists called for a world revolution to bring an end to both the war and the capitalist system, and found sympathetic followers in many nations. In Germany, Hungary, and Italy, left-wing revolutionaries inspired by the Bolshevik Revolution tried unsuccessfully to seize power in 1919–20.

At the same time extremist movements on the right sought to crush the left-wing challenge by installing their own dictatorial regimes. In Italy, an unscrupulous politician named Benito Mussolini promised to restore to his country the glory and power of ancient Rome. Mussolini built a movement known as fascism. It combined extreme nationalism and anticommunism with contempt for democratic government.

Mussolini, known as Il Duce, leads fascists in honoring the flag.
(Library of Congress)

When Mussolini came to power in 1922 he used terrorist tactics and repressive laws to stamp out opposition to his rule.

In Germany during the 1920s a political fanatic named Adolf Hitler dreamed of duplicating Mussolini's success. Hitler had fought in his country's army in the First World War as a common soldier. He had been decorated for bravery and wounded in action. Like many other German veterans, he returned home with the delusion that Germany lost the war only because its army had been betrayed—"stabbed in the back," a popular saying went—by its civilian leaders. Hitler was a man possessed by fierce hatreds. After the war he discovered he had the ability to get others to share his obsessions. Germany must wipe out the shame of its defeat and restore its national greatness, Hitler shouted to his followers in the National Socialist German Workers Party—the Nazis. They could do this by driving out of public life the Jews, the communists, and the leaders who had founded the new German republic in 1918.

The new German democracy was fatally undermined by the harsh peace imposed on the country by its opponents. The Treaty of Versailles (named for the town in France where it was drawn up) had been signed by the victorious allies in 1919. Only the United States did not sign, because the treaty failed to win Senate approval. The treaty stripped Germany of its overseas colonies and some of its border territories, restricted the size of its army and navy, and required its government to make reparation payments to Britain and France for the costs of the war. The German economy was already nearly bankrupt as a result of four years of war, and the reparations made a bad situation worse. Inflation and unemployment led to mass suffering and lent credibility to Hitler's ideas.

In 1923 the Nazis attempted to seize power in Germany in an unsuccessful coup, sometimes referred to as the "Beer Hall Putsch" because it was plotted in a Munich beer hall. Arrested by the authorities and briefly imprisoned, Hitler wrote his autobiography, *Mein Kampf (My Struggle)*. The book was widely read in Germany but, unfortunately, ignored by most of the rest of the world. In *Mein Kampf* Hitler outlined his plans for a dictatorship in Germany powerful enough to enforce racial "purification" at home, while pushing eastward to gain *Lebensraum* (living room) for the German population. Germany's "Aryan" race, he argued, was destined for world leadership. "Inferior" eastern European races, like the Poles, Ukrainians, Russians,

The Versailles Settlement
and the Rise of Nazism

WORLD WAR I ENDED IN STAGES. THE FIGHTING stopped with the armistice agreed to by the Western allies (the United States, Britain, and France) and the Central Powers (Germany and Austria-Hungary) on November 11, 1918. But it was not until the following spring that the victorious powers drew up a peace treaty in Versailles, France, which the Germans were compelled to sign under threat of continued economic blockade and renewed hostilities. Under the provisions of the Versailles settlement, the Germans had to admit their nation's guilt for starting the war and agree to pay financial reparations to France, Belgium, and Britain for its costs. The provinces of Alsace and Lorraine on Germany's western frontier were given to France (which had lost control of the districts in the Franco-Prussian war of 1870–71). In the east, Poland was awarded a land corridor to the sea that cut through eastern Prussia. Germany also had to agree to severe limitations on the size of its military forces.

Both German pride and the German economy were wounded by the harsh provisions of the Versailles settlement, and the Nazis were able to play on the resulting German sense of grievance in their own rise to power. Adolf Hitler repudiated the treaty in 1935, and the territorial demands he began making in eastern and central Europe were, in the words of Nazi propagandists, intended to undo the "crime of Versailles."

and Jews, would have to be pushed aside and crushed if they stood in the way of Germany's destiny.

Germany's economic problems temporarily lessened in the late 1920s but returned with the onset of the worldwide Great Depression in 1929. While Nazi strong-arm squads, known as stormtroopers, attacked political opponents in the streets, Nazi parliamentary candidates attracted the support of increasing numbers of German voters. Finally, through a combination of both violent and legal means, Hitler took over as Germany's chancellor in March 1933. Acting with greater ruthlessness by far than Mussolini, he turned Germany into a totalitarian dictatorship where he ruled and was worshiped as the absolute leader, or *Führer*. Once in power, Hitler put into practice the promises

BACKGROUND TO WAR

he had made in *Mein Kampf.* He rearmed Germany in violation of the Versailles Treaty, enacted a series of laws discriminating against Germany's Jewish population, and launched a new and aggressive foreign policy that by the spring of 1939 had brought Germany control of Austria and Czechoslovakia.

Hitler found some allies abroad. The most powerful were Fascist Italy (which had launched its own war of conquest against Ethiopia in 1935 and annexed Albania in 1939) and, on the other side of the world, imperial Japan. Japan, a crowded island nation with limited natural resources, had been expanding its power on the Asian mainland since the start of the 20th century. Japan had an emperor, Hirohito, and a civilian cabinet that ruled in his name. Increasingly, however, the real power to make decisions, especially in foreign policy, lay with an ambitious group of army officers. In 1931 these officers provoked an incident in the northern Chinese province of Manchuria. They used it

Hitler (third from right) and his inner circle pose for the camera at giant Nuremberg rally. *(Library of Congress)*

His Imperial Japanese Majesty
Hirohito *(National Archives)*

as the excuse to conquer the province and convert it into a pro-Japanese puppet state called Manchukuo.

Without ever formally declaring war, the Japanese kept up a steady pressure on China's weak central government, grabbing more and more of China's territory. In 1937 the Japanese army began a drive that in a few months' time brought all of China's major coastal cities under its control. The Japanese also launched probing attacks on the Soviet border, but after a series of bloody defeats drew back from further northward expansion. Japan's future, its leaders decided, lay in consolidating its hold on China and expanding its power into Southeast Asia (an area rich in such resources as oil, rubber, and rice). As the 1930s came to an end, Japanese leaders were reluctant to provoke the western European powers, with their colonies in Southeast Asia, and the United States, which ruled over the Philippines. But given the right opportunity, they decided they would strike, and strike hard, to obtain their goals.

The half-hearted diplomatic countermeasures enacted by other nations could not turn back the tide of German, Italian, and Japanese aggression. The League of Nations, the organization established by the Versailles treaty to monitor international behavior, condemned Japan's war in Manchuria—and Italy's war in Ethiopia—but to no avail. Because of England and France's appeasement policies, Germany carried out its expansive strategy without reprisal. Meanwhile the three aggressors formed closer links among themselves. In the Spanish Civil War of 1936–39, Hitler and Mussolini united to back a military uprising that installed Generalissimo Francisco Franco as dictator of Spain. Mussolini announced the existence of a "Rome-Berlin Axis" in 1936, meaning that Germany and Italy considered themselves part of a united coalition. Japan formally joined the Axis in 1940, and the three countries were thereafter known as the Axis powers.

Germany, Italy, and Japan harbored similar ambitions to expand their own territory and power, and they confronted some of the same enemies. Yet they were never completely united in their military and political strategy. Despite the charges of Allied wartime

The Spanish Civil War
TRIAL RUN FOR WORLD WAR II

IN JULY 1936 SPANISH MILITARY FORCES UNDER THE command of Generalissimo Francisco Franco attempted to overthrow the democratically elected Republican government of Spain. The uprising failed, but a full-scale civil war then broke out between the Loyalists who backed the Republic, and the Nationalist forces that backed Franco's revolt.

The Spanish Civil War was an international as well as a national conflict. It proved a dress rehearsal for World War II. The European fascist dictators, Hitler and Mussolini, rushed troops and arms to aid Franco. The Germans used Spain as a testing ground for the terror tactics they would soon unleash on civilian populations across Europe, most infamously in the destruction of the village of Guernica by Nazi bombers in 1937. The Soviet Union and Mexico backed the Republic, and some 30,000 foreign volunteers (including about 3,000 from the United States) fought in the communist-organized International Brigades on the Loyalist side. France and England, bent on appeasing the fascist dictators, vowed not to get involved with their neighbor's plight. Both countries forbade the sale of arms to the Republic, as did the isolationist United States.

In January 1939, as Franco's forces closed in on the last remaining Loyalist strongholds in Spain, President Roosevelt mused in a meeting of his cabinet about the "grave mistake" that the United States had made in failing to come to the aid of the Loyalists, with arms and other support. Republican Spain, he declared, should have been given "what she needed to fight for her life against Franco—to fight for her life and for the lives of some of the rest of us as well, as events will very likely prove." Madrid, Spain's capital, fell to the Nationalists in March 1939. World War II broke out six months later.

EUROPE, AUGUST 1939

■	Axis powers
▧	Protectorates of Germany
▨	Annexed by Germany
▒	Annexed by Italy
▤	Neutral powers

1 March 1935
Saar Basin to Germany
by plebiscite

2 March 1936
Rhineland remilitarized

3 March 1938
Austria annexed
by Germany

4 October 1938
to Hungary

5 October 1938
Occupied by Germany

6 March 1939
Occupied by Germany

7 March 1939
to Hungary

8 March 1939
Annexed by Germany

9 April 1939
Albania occupied
by Italy

10 April 1939
Russo-German
non-aggression pact

11 May 1939
"Pact of Steel"

propaganda, the Axis powers did not have any master plan to start the Second World War and conquer the world. While Germany went to war in September 1939, Italy did not join the conflict until April 1940. The Japanese would remain officially at peace until December 1941. But the leaders of each country, pursuing their own separate ambitions, together brought about the most destructive war in the history of the world.

It was a war that the United States, at first, was determined to sit out. But even though the United States remained neutral, the war preoccupied President Roosevelt. It especially filled his calendar after the Germans conquered Poland in September 1939. It was not until October 11 that he had an hour to spare for Leo Szilard and Albert Einstein's messenger, Alexander Sachs. When Sachs met with Roosevelt in the White House, he handed him Einstein's letter, and also made some remarks of his own on recent developments in nuclear physics. When he saw that Roosevelt's attention was beginning to wander, Sachs asked if they might meet again the next day. Roosevelt suggested he join him for breakfast.

The next morning Sachs told Roosevelt a story about the 19th-century French emperor Napoleon Bonaparte. Bonaparte had received a letter from an American inventor, who tried to interest him in a new kind of ship that had no need for sails to cross the ocean. The great emperor could not be bothered with the fantasies of technological dreamers and dismissed the offer.

The young American in question, Sachs told the president, was Robert Fulton, who went on to invent the steamboat. Roosevelt was a man often impatient with detail, but Sachs now had the president's full attention.

Sachs continued his briefing on nuclear fission, concluding with a prediction by a British physicist that someday soon men would learn how to release "the almost infinite power" of atomic energy. "We cannot prevent him from doing so," Sachs said, quoting the physicist, "and can only hope that he will not use it exclusively in blowing up his next-door neighbor." Roosevelt got the point. "Alex, what you are after is

President Franklin Delano Roosevelt *(Library of Congress)*

to see that the Nazis don't blow us up." "Precisely," replied Sachs. Roosevelt called in an aide, held up the documents that Sachs had brought with him from Einstein and Szilard, and declared, "This requires action!"

In war, few things are ever quite so simple and straightforward as they at first seem. It would take another two years before the United States launched a serious program of atomic weapons research. Then it took an additional three and a half years before, in July 1945, scientists exploded the first atomic bomb at Los Alamos testing ground in New Mexico. By that time Hitler was dead and Nazi Germany defeated, but the bomb would be used in the climactic act of the Second World War, when it was dropped on the Japanese cities of Hiroshima and Nagasaki.

For most of 1939 Leo Szilard and his fellow refugee scientists had tried, desperately and naively, to find someone in authority willing to listen to them. They were scorned and ignored, but in the end, for better or worse, they unloosed an idea that would change the world. Before that would come to pass, however, the United States would have to join with many other nations in the most horrendous war the world had ever experienced.

3

AMERICA'S ROAD TO WAR

Sheltered behind wide ocean frontiers, the United States had avoided involvement in European conflicts for nearly the first century and a half of its national existence. American entry into the First World War in 1917 had broken that isolationist tradition, but in the 1920s it seemed as though the United States had resumed its earlier hands-off stance. American diplomats were busy in those years drawing up a series of multinational antiwar treaties, among them the 1928 Kellogg-Briand Pact. In this agreement, 15 nations, including the United States, Great Britain, France, and Germany, swore they would no longer engage in war "as an instrument of national policy in their relations with one another." Otherwise, Americans remained disappointed with the results of a world war that had failed to "make the world safe for democracy," as they had been promised it would. In the years since 1918, Americans had made it clear to their elected officials that they wanted no entanglement in Europe's problems.

After taking office in 1933, President Roosevelt was preoccupied with solving economic problems at home. He found it easy to go along with the isolationist mood of the American public. By 1937 European and Asian developments proved increasingly difficult for him to ignore. There was little he could do, however, to express his concern about the growing aggressiveness of German, Italian, and Japanese foreign policy.

Responding to pressure from the voters, Congress passed a series of laws in the mid-1930s known as the Neutrality Acts. These were

Charles Lindbergh and "America First" Isolationism

CHARLES LINDBERGH, A DARING STUNT FLYER, WON international fame at the age of 25 in 1927, when he successfully piloted his single-engine plane, *The Spirit of St. Louis,* nonstop from New York to Paris, the first solo crossing of the Atlantic. He was lionized by his fellow citizens as "Lucky Lindy" and the "Lone Eagle," a symbol of American daring and mechanical know-how.

In the 1930s, Lindbergh observed the growth of German air power with apprehension. He became convinced that Hitler was invincible, and that America should stay out of any future European war. He was by no means alone in such beliefs; Congress passed a series of laws in the 1930s designed to insure U.S. neutrality. When President Roosevelt proposed to revise these laws in the fall of 1939 to allow Britain to purchase U.S. arms, Lindbergh emerged as one of his bitterest critics. In dozens of speeches over the next two years, Lindbergh rallied public opposition to any American aid for Britain.

In 1940 isolationists banded together into the America First Committee, claiming 850,000 members nationwide. Speaking on behalf of the organization, Lindbergh accused President Roosevelt of seeking "world domination." In his most notorious speech, delivered in September 1941, just three months before Pearl Harbor, Lindbergh warned that American Jews were behind the growing pressure for U.S. entry into the war. Lindbergh denied harboring pro-Nazi sentiments, but as his rhetoric grew more extreme his heroic stature grew increas-

intended to avoid a repetition of the events of 1917. Back then the issue of the sinking of American ships and the loss of American lives to German U-boats (submarines) in the Atlantic had served to rally the country to go to war. The Neutrality Act of 1935 called for the embargo, or prohibition, of arms shipments to foreign nations involved in war, regardless of U.S. sympathies for either side in the war. Acts passed in the next few years made it illegal for American bankers to make loans to nations at war and forbade American passengers from traveling on ships owned by belligerent powers. Congress declared that even non-military goods could be sold to warring nations only on a "cash and carry" basis. The idea was that, since American ships would not be used

ingly tarnished. President Roosevelt himself privately fumed that Lindbergh's speeches could have been "written by [Nazi propaganda chief] Goebbels himself."

Shortly after the attack on Pearl Harbor on December 7, 1941, America First disbanded. Lindbergh fell into obscurity. But in a gesture of his restoration to public favor after the war ended, President Eisenhower appointed him a brigadier general in the U.S. Air Force Reserve in 1954.

Charles A. Lindbergh, standing alongside an airplane, 1929.
(Library of Congress)

to transport these goods across the ocean, they would not be at risk of sinking by hostile submarines.

Embargoes imposed under the provisions of the Neutrality Acts kept the United States from providing arms to Ethiopia in 1935, and to the Spanish Republic during the Civil War of 1936–39. On October 5, 1937, responding to German and Italian intervention in Spain and the renewed Japanese offensive in China, Roosevelt delivered a speech. He denounced such acts of international lawlessness and called on "peace-loving nations" to "quarantine" the aggressors. So mindful was he of the strength of isolationist sentiment in the United States that he did not name the aggressors he had in mind. Neither did he propose any actions for the United States or other governments to take in order to carry out this quarantine. Yet even this mild statement aroused a storm of protest.

When war did break out in Europe in September 1939, Roosevelt spoke to the American people over the radio, declaring the nation's official neutrality. Then he added: "I cannot ask that every American remain neutral in thought as well. Even a neutral cannot be asked to close his mind or his conscience." Most Americans were, in fact, anti-Nazi. Public opinion polls revealed overwhelming sympathy for the British and French—along with equally overwhelming majorities in favor of the United States remaining out of the war. After a bitter debate, Congress did agree to amend the earlier Neutrality Acts. Under the revised law passed on November 4, 1939, U.S. manufacturers were once again permitted to sell arms to belligerents, but only on a "cash and carry" basis. This meant that the United States would now supply weapons to the anti-Nazi Allies. Those nations, however, still had to pay for the weapons up front and use their own ships to carry them back across the Atlantic.

Even though the United States remained neutral for the next two years, the issue of the war soon dominated American politics. The United States became increasingly divided. The interventionists argued that America's own national interests required coming to the aid of Hitler's opponents. The isolationists argued that such intervention would only lead to the futile spilling of American blood. The most powerful isolationist group was the America First Committee, which at the peak of its strength claimed more than 850,000 members nationwide.

In the first six months of the war, occasionally referred to at the time as the "phony war," little fighting took place on the western front in Europe. In the east the Nazi *Blitzkrieg* ("lightning war") had rolled over Polish defenses in a few weeks. In the west, French and German troops stared at each other across their frontier fortifications, while hardly ever exchanging a shot. But in the spring of 1940, the Germans unleashed a new blitzkrieg, this time in the west. They conquered Norway, Denmark, Belgium, Holland, and France, all in a matter of three months, while forcing the emergency evacuation of the British army from the European continent. By mid-June, the Germans were parading triumphantly through Paris. Britain and its empire stood alone against the Nazis.

London in the blitz: buildings destroyed by firebombs tumble into ruins; St. Paul's Cathedral, in background, survived. *(Library of Congress)*

Hitler had achieved in one springtime, and at a minimal cost in German manpower, what the kaiser had failed to achieve in four years of bloody war, from 1914 to 1918. With the start of the Battle of Britain, Hitler's aerial assault on British airfields and cities, many Americans feared that Britain would be the next victim to fall prey to Nazi aggression. In reality, by the autumn of 1940 Hitler had once again shifted his attention eastward, making plans for an invasion of the Soviet Union the following spring. But with London already in flames, it was easy for

Americans to imagine German bombers appearing next over New York or Washington, D.C.

With the fall of France, Roosevelt began to call for all-out aid to Britain—but not for sending American troops overseas. He was still careful to present each proposed new step toward U.S. involvement in the war in terms of defending the American continent against foreign attack. Sometimes he acted on his own. In the "destroyer deal" of September 2, 1940, the president signed an executive order trading 50 U.S. destroyers for leases on naval and air bases located in British possessions in the Western Hemisphere, including Newfoundland, Bermuda, and the Bahamas. Sometimes he was able to drag a reluctant Congress along with him. On September 16, 1940, Roosevelt signed a bill passed by Congress establishing the first compulsory peacetime draft, a major step toward American mobilization for war. The bill was good only for one year, and when it came up for Congress's consideration in 1941 it was renewed by a margin of only a single vote. Repeatedly the president went before the country, assuring the voters that he did not seek or foresee any direct American military involvement in the war. As he declared on October 30, 1940, shortly before the end of that fall's presidential election campaign, "I have said this before, but I shall say it again and again and again: Your boys are not going to be sent into any foreign wars."

Safely reelected for an unprecedented third term in office in November, Roosevelt called for more dramatic steps to provide aid to Britain. Responding to a letter from Prime Minister Winston Churchill warning that Britain had run out of cash reserves to pay for U.S. arms, Roosevelt proposed a new plan on December 17, 1940; it was called lend-lease. If a neighbor's house was on fire, he argued, it would make sense to lend him your garden hose to prevent the fire from spreading to your own property. In a similar fashion the United States should now be prepared to "lend" the weapons of war to those fighting the Nazis. He still insisted that this was a way to defeat Germany without direct U.S. military involvement. Instead, the United States would become "the great arsenal of democracy."

Public opinion was finally shifting in the direction of the president's policies. Polls showed that 70 percent of the U.S. public now favored all aid to Britain short of a declaration of war. Isolationist opponents in Congress charged that passage of the Lend-Lease Act would result in U.S. involvement in a war in which "every fourth American boy [would be] plowed under." Still, the bill passed both houses of Congress and was signed into law by Roosevelt on March 11, 1941. Lend-lease aid worth more than $27 billion, including guns, tanks, aircraft, ships, food, and other necessities, would be provided to 38 countries by the end of war. Great Britain received the largest amount, followed by the Soviet Union, which became part of the anti-Nazi coalition after its invasion by Nazi troops on June 22, 1941.

Whatever the president chose to say in public to assure nervous Americans, by the spring of 1941 it was clearly only a matter of time before the United States fully entered the war. Secret talks between American and British military officers were held in Washington in the spring of 1941. These led to an agreement that in the event of war breaking out with both Germany and Japan, the United States and Britain would make the defeat of Germany their priority. Meanwhile, the Japanese took advantage of France's defeat in Europe to force the French government to accept the stationing of Japanese troops in French colonies in Indochina. Roosevelt placed a freeze on Japanese assets in the United States and embargoed the sale of American oil and scrap iron to Japan. U.S. troops were sent to the North Atlantic to occupy Greenland in April and Iceland in July, not only to guard against German seizure but also to provide U.S. naval bases in those vital shipping lanes.

The first American ship to be sunk in the war, the merchant vessel *Robin Moor,* was torpedoed by a German U-boat in the Atlantic Ocean on May 21, 1941. Hitler was dismayed, because he was still hoping that the United States would stay out of the war. Beginning in July, the U.S. Navy operated a regular antisubmarine patrol in the western half of the Atlantic. That new policy led to a battle in North Atlantic waters on September 4 between the USS *Greer* and a German submarine, although the exchange of torpedoes and depth charges left no damage on either side. Later investigations would show that it was the *Greer* that had actually initiated the confrontation. Roosevelt used the incident, however, to issue a "shoot-on sight" order for U.S. naval vessels in the Atlantic whenever they came across German U-boats.

For the next few months the U.S. Navy was engaged in an undeclared naval war with the German navy. Eleven U.S. sailors died on October 17, when a U-boat torpedoed the destroyer USS *Kearny,* accompanying a British merchant convoy. These sailors were the first U.S. military casualties of World War II. Two weeks later 115 sailors aboard the destroyer

Prime Minister Winston Churchill attends to correspondence in his private railcar. *(Library of Congress)*

Reuben James lost their lives when their ship was sunk by the Germans. Congress responded by once again amending the Neutrality Act. It now permitted arming of U.S. merchant ships and allowed them to carry goods into war zones.

Some Americans urged the president to declare war after the first American sailors lost their lives in the icy waters of the North Atlantic. But the isolationists had by no means lost all their influence, and Roosevelt did not want to lead a divided country into war. Sooner or later, he believed, the Nazis would provide him with a suitable reason to go before Congress and ask for a declaration of war. So Roosevelt continued to hold back as 1941 was drawing to a close.

Just as he expected, a blow was soon to be delivered that would give the country a rallying cry to unite behind. What the president and his military advisers did not expect was the direction from which it was to come. On November 26, 1941, a Japanese naval striking force of six aircraft carriers, two battleships, and a host of smaller supporting vessels set sail from a port in the Japanese Kurile Islands. Maintaining absolute radio silence, this force headed east on a little-traveled route through the North Pacific. Their top-secret destination was Pearl Harbor in Hawaii, home base for the U.S. Pacific fleet. When planes from the Japanese carriers suddenly appeared in the sky over Pearl Harbor on Sunday morning, December 7, 1941, the era of American isolationism came to a dramatic end.

4

DEFEAT IN
THE PACIFIC

On December 2, the Japanese fleet steaming toward Hawaii received a message from headquarters: "Climb Mount Niitaka." Vice Adm. Chuichi Nagumo, commander of the fleet, knew what that meant. There was to be no turning back. Pearl Harbor, home base to the U.S. Pacific fleet, would be bombed on the morning of December 7. The plan to attack Pearl Harbor had been conceived by Adm. Isoroku Yamamoto, commander in chief of the Japanese navy. A brilliant strategist, Yamamoto had recognized years earlier the importance of air power in naval warfare. Thanks to his influence, the Japanese navy built a powerful striking force of aircraft carriers. By attacking the American fleet Yamamoto hoped to give the Japanese six months to secure their control over a large area of Southeast Asia and the western Pacific Ocean.

Already, other Japanese battleships and troop transport ships were moving toward different destinations. The Japanese planned to follow their attack at Pearl Harbor with assaults on the Philippines, Burma, Malaya, the Dutch East Indies, New Guinea, and key island strongholds like Guam and Wake. The oil, rubber, and other resources of Southeast Asia would soon be at their disposal. They would then establish a defensive perimeter of fortified islands and aircraft carriers. Japanese leaders hoped that the United States would decide that all-out war against Japan would be too costly—especially if, as seemed likely, the United States was drawn into war with Nazi Germany at the same time. Then, perhaps, America would settle for a negotiated peace. It was a gamble,

Prime Minister
and War Minister
of Japan Hideki
Tojo (bottom)
(National Archives)

with life and death stakes. Everything hinged on the outcome at Pearl Harbor. The pilots aboard the Japanese aircraft carriers in the early morning hours of December 7 asked heaven to bless their mission. They would not be disappointed, at least in the short run.

The first wave of 189 high-altitude bombers, dive bombers, and torpedo planes took off from the six Japanese carriers at 6 A.M. and headed south toward the Hawaiian island of Oahu. As the pilots flew across the ocean, they nervously watched for American reconnaissance planes or intercepting fighters. None were seen. A few minutes before 8 A.M. they approached the base at Pearl Harbor. There they were astonished to see the American fleet spread out below them—lying peacefully at anchor, with no fighter planes in the air and no antiaircraft guns firing. The bombers, which headed for the army air bases at Hickam and Wheeler fields, saw hundreds of American planes lined up on the ground wingtip to wingtip, completely immobilized. The Japanese flight leader radioed back to his fleet commander the agreed-upon code words, *"Tora! Tora! Tora!"* (Tiger, Tiger, Tiger). This meant that the attack would be a total surprise.

In the years after December 7, 1941, congressional and military investigators, journalists, and historians all tried to explain why the United States was so unprepared for the Japanese assault. In fact, both in Washington, D.C., and in American military headquarters in Hawaii, almost everyone in a position of authority knew that the Japanese planned to go to war within a matter of days. In Washington, American intelligence analysts had learned how to read the top secret Japanese diplomatic code. On December 6 they had decoded a message from Tokyo to Japan's Washington embassy. This instructed the Japanese ambassador to break off negotiations with the U.S. secretary of state the following afternoon. When President Roosevelt was notified, he explained "This means war!" On Sunday morning Gen. George Marshall, the American chief of staff, sent a message to American bases in the Panama Canal, San Francisco, the Philippines, and Hawaii warning of the imminence of war. The message did not reach the American commander at Pearl Harbor until it was too late. In any case, American commanders on the scene had long considered the possibility of a surprise Japanese attack.

But somehow all of this advance knowledge did the defenders of Pearl Harbor no good. American military commanders had not taken even such elementary steps as placing torpedo nets in the narrow channel that led to the berthed American warships. Nor had they sent out any reconnaissance flights north of Hawaii on December 6. They underestimated their enemy, and the American fleet would pay a bitter price for such mistakes.

Even on the morning of December 7, there were warnings that, if heeded, would have given Pearl Harbor nearly an hour to prepare for the attack. Shortly after 7 A.M. a U.S. destroyer sank a Japanese midget submarine near the entrance to Pearl Harbor. About the same time, U.S. radar bases on Hawaii called in a sighting of unexplained blips on their radar screens. But the report from the destroyer was ignored by navy officers as "unverified." Meanwhile, an army officer assured the radar

DEFEAT IN THE PACIFIC

operators that the blips on their screens were made by American planes due to arrive from California.

Within minutes after the arrival of the first wave of Japanese attackers, Pearl Harbor became a scene of horror, destruction, and confusion. The pride of the Pacific fleet, including the battleships *West Virginia, Oklahoma, California,* and *Arizona,* were all hit by torpedoes in the first few minutes of the raid. The *Oklahoma* capsized, trapping many of its crew in air pockets within the ship. (Thirty-two would be rescued the next day by workers who cut through the hull with oxyacetylene torches). An armor-piercing bomb hit the second gun turret of the *Arizona,* setting off explosions from forward ammunition magazines.

Destroyer USS *Shaw* explodes during the Japanese raid on Pearl Harbor, December 7, 1941. *(National Archives)*

WORLD WAR II

Rescuers on a motor launch take on survivors from torpedoed battleship USS *West Virginia*—one of six battleships sunk on Sunday morning, December 7, 1941. *(Library of Congress)*

Flames from the *Arizona* set the *Tennessee* ablaze. The air filled with thick black smoke while burning oil spread across the harbor waters.

The first wave of Japanese planes dropped their bombs and torpedoes with ease. With bombs dropping all around them, American fighter planes were unable to get off the ground. Aboard ships, sailors ran to get ammunition for their antiaircraft guns, and found they could not get into the locked ammunition cabinets. By the time the second wave of bombers arrived, at 8:40 A.M., the Americans were able to put up more resistance.

When the attack ended, however, only two hours after it had started, there could be no doubt that it had been an overwhelming Japanese victory. At a cost of only 29 planes shot down, the Japanese had been able to sink or badly damage 18 U.S. ships, including eight battleships. They destroyed 180 planes on the ground and damaged many others. Twenty-four hundred U.S. sailors, marines, and soldiers (and 68 civilians) had been killed, including more than 1,000 Americans aboard the *Arizona,* one of the two battleships left beyond repair. (The ship remains where it sank on December 7, a permanent memorial to the Americans who lost their lives that day.)

Only two things kept the attack from being a total disaster for the American cause in the Pacific. One was that all three of the Pacific fleet's aircraft carriers and seven of its heavy cruisers happened to be elsewhere and were thus spared. Also, the Japanese had failed to destroy the base's oil storage tanks and maintenance facilities. This meant that Pearl Harbor could continue to be used by the surviving ships of the fleet. Had the Japanese sent in another wave or two of attacking planes, they might have forced the Pacific fleet to retreat all the way back to the West Coast.

It was 2:25 on a Sunday afternoon in Washington, D.C., when the wire services sent a seven-word announcement over the news tickers: "White House says Japs attack Pearl Harbor." Radio announcers all over the country interrupted their regular broadcasts to tell Americans that they were at war. In some West Coast cities, panic broke out, with wild rumors circulating about enemy submarines sighted offshore and enemy planes flying overhead. That night air raid alarms sounded in Los Angeles and San Francisco. Mobs in the streets attempted to enforce their own "blackout" by throwing rocks at streetlights.

Just after noon on December 8, President Roosevelt went before a joint session of Congress to ask for a declaration of war. He began his five-minute-long speech by declaring: "Yesterday, December 7, 1941—a date that will live in infamy—the United States of America was suddenly and deliberately attacked by naval and air forces of the Empire of Japan." Roosevelt got his declaration of war with unanimous approval in the Senate and only one dissenting vote in the House of Representatives, Jeannette Rarkin of Missouri. Senator Burton Wheeler, one of the leaders of the isolationists in the Senate, declared, "The only thing to do now is to lick hell out of them." Roosevelt did not mention Germany or Italy in his message to Congress, but Hitler and Mussolini supported their Asian Axis partner by declaring war on the United States on December 11. The U.S. Congress then declared war on these two nations also.

Within hours of their assault on Pearl Harbor, the Japanese had also attacked the Philippines, Malaya, and Hong Kong. In the Philippines, as

at Pearl Harbor, the Japanese were able to take the defenders by sur-
prise. They destroyed on the ground most of the American planes avail-
able for the defense of the islands. Japanese destroyers shelled the
American base on Midway Island on December 7, but made no further
effort, for the moment, to take the island. The U.S. Marines stationed on
Guam and Wake were not so lucky. Guam fell on December 12. Wake
Island came under air assault on December 8, beat off an attempted
Japanese landing on December 11 and sank two Japanese destroyers.
The brave defenders of Wake won the admiration of the American public, still reeling from the news at Pearl Harbor. One story widely
repeated in the United States was that the marine commander on Wake
had radioed "Send us more Japs" after the first enemy landing was
turned back. (It had no basis in fact.) The Japanese kept up a steady aerial bombardment of Wake and made a second landing on December
22. When it became clear that no U.S. relief force would arrive in time
to save the island, the garrison surrendered on December 23.

Small detachments of Japanese troops began landing at scattered
locations in the Philippines on December 8. They followed with a full-
scale landing on Luzon, the most important Philippine island, on
December 22. Gen. Douglas MacArthur, commander of U.S. Armed
Forces in the Far East, had a force of more than 100,000 Filipino and
American troops under his command to repel the Japanese invaders.
Many of the Filipinos were poorly trained, and the army as a whole was
poorly equipped. MacArthur, a vain man who loved publicity, was
known for carrying around a riding crop and smoking a large corncob
pipe. He made the mistake of spreading his troops and supplies over too
wide an area, hoping to confront and defeat the Japanese as they landed
on the beaches. But the Japanese had better troops and enjoyed air
superiority. They swiftly moved inland, driving MacArthur's forces
toward the capital city of Manila.

MacArthur was forced to change plans. He pulled his troops back
into a more defensible position, where they could hold out until help
could arrive from the United States. American and Filipino troops
retreated to the 25-mile-long Bataan Peninsula, which stretches into the
ocean at the west side of Manila Bay. The other American strong point,
where MacArthur made his headquarters, was the heavily fortified
island of Corregidor in Manila Bay.

The rugged landscape of Bataan favored the defenders, but they
were in no physical condition to put up a strong fight. MacArthur had

ignored prewar plans for stockpiling six months' worth of food on Bataan in the event of an outbreak of war. Instead, when 80,000 American and Filipino soldiers (along with an additional 26,000 civilians) made it to the peninsula, they found only limited food reserves waiting for them. Japanese ships and planes cut off Bataan's defenders from resupply. Hunger and disease took as many casualties among the defenders as did the repeated Japanese artillery and infantry assaults. Still, they held out into the new year. They hoped for the return of an American fleet carrying the planes, reinforcements, and supplies they would need to strike back at the Japanese. But as the weeks passed, in the dark new year of 1942, it became apparent that the Americans and Filipinos hoped in vain.

5

MOBILIZING FOR WAR

In the early days of 1942 a spirit of unity gripped the nation. It was best summed up by the slogan "Remember Pearl Harbor." But the outcome of wars is not decided by the strength or purity of patriotic sentiments alone. It takes modern weapons and those who know how to use them to best advantage, and both were in short supply in December 1941. The United States faced vast problems in assembling, training, and equipping its new military forces. The last time Americans had gone to war was back in 1917. That war had ended before the bulk of the U.S. Army had been able to get overseas, let alone see any real combat. This time would be different.

When war broke out in Europe in 1939, the U.S. Army had only 188,000 troops. This was a force smaller than the military might available to some of the least important European powers, such as Bulgaria. In September 1940 Congress passed a bill establishing the Selective Service System, which represented the nation's first peacetime draft. The first draftees entered the army in November 1940. More than 600,000 had been drafted by the middle of 1941. Ten million men would be drafted by all services by the end of the war. Another 5 million, including women as well as men, enlisted voluntarily.

At first only the army, the largest wing of the military services, took draftees. Starting in 1942 the navy and marines did so as well. In 1940 all men ages 21 to 35 were made eligible for the draft. Later on, as the military's manpower needs increased, the lower age limit was dropped to 18 and the upper age limit raised to 38. Local draft boards chose which men were to go into the military. They were authorized to give deferments to men who were physically or mentally incapable of service. They could also offer deferments to married men and those with children (although fathers also began to be drafted in 1943). In order to keep the nation's vital flow of food and weapons from being disrupted, draft boards could defer farmers and workers employed in war industries.

Receiving a notice of induction from a local draft board did not guarantee military service. The army's own doctors in the first year of the draft rejected nearly one-third of all draftees for physical defects. These initial high standards could not be kept. Rather than reject men for such things as rotten or missing teeth, the army expanded its dental services. By 1945 the army's 25,000 dentists had fitted soldiers with 2,500,000 sets of dentures. The army also began accepting nearsighted and even one-eyed men, illiterates, and convicted criminals. Of course the vast majority of draftees did not suffer from such handicaps. In the first two years of the war the army created 90 new divisions (troops that trained and then fought together). After 1943 soldiers were trained as replacements for existing units.

New draftees were first sent to reception centers. There they were poked and prodded by the doctors, given their shots, and issued uniforms. The clothing and equipment they received was "government issue," or GI, which is how the term *GI* began to be applied to American soldiers. From reception centers they were sent to camps for basic training, which usually took about eight weeks. Advanced training, exercises, and maneuvers could extend the time a soldier spent in preparing to fight. It took a year to train a pilot for combat. The basic trainee's life was not an easy one. They were up at 5:30 A.M., facing a day of training that could stretch up to 16 hours, six days a week. They sat through lectures on everything from first aid to military courtesy. They took 25-mile hikes with heavy packs, ran obstacle courses, and learned how to take apart and reassemble their weapons with blindfolds on. KP (kitchen police), garbage detail, or latrine duty might all be added onto their regular training day. All this was compensated by a private's pay of $21 a month (later raised to $50).

At first, the military training camps were poorly run. Army officers struggled to cope with the vast numbers of new draftees who were flooding in. "Hurry up and wait" became a motto for every new soldier as he learned to stand in line for food and equipment, or sit around waiting for scarce transportation. Manufacturers were slow to shift

U.S. Army Engineer Corps soldiers in training carry some heavy equipment for the construction of a bridge or pier, Fort Belvoir, Virginia, 1942. *(Library of Congress)*

from civilian production to what they saw as the uncertain profits of military production. In mid-1940 only 7 percent of American production was devoted to defense. By the time of the attack on Pearl Harbor that figure had grown to 25 percent, but it was still impossible to satisfy the needs of the vastly expanded armed forces. Draftees destined for the infantry trained with broomsticks instead of rifles. Potential artillerymen had to line up to get a chance to fire the few workable pieces of artillery available for training.

Gradually the amount and quality of materials available to the soldiers improved. Clothing and equipment evolved to meet the needs revealed by overseas combat. Leather-soled boots rotted in jungle climates and were replaced by rubber-soled boots. The cloth leggings U.S. soldiers had wound around their calves were abandoned as army boots were redesigned to fit higher on the leg. The 1917-vintage, British-style "tin helmet" gave way to the now familiar rounded helmet with helmet liner. Many of the cumbersome Enfield and Springfield rifles first given to the draftees had been made before the First World War. They were replaced by the semiautomatic M-1 Garand rifle as the standard infantry weapon. The C ration and K ration that were issued to soldiers when they went into combat were improved (not that many soldiers would ever admit it). Army nutritionists discovered the foods that the soldiers absolutely refused to eat. A kind of canned meat and vegetable hash proved particularly unpopular, as did instant lemonade. Instant coffee, on the other hand, proved so popular that after the war it gained a wide civilian market.

Many combat veterans later complained that their training had been too hurried or that they had been too tired to pay attention. They also pointed out that too many of the subjects taught had been irrelevant to the actual challenges they faced in battle. But what military training did manage to do was to break down the barriers between soldiers, making the different kinds of life they had led as civilians seem unimportant. Training created among them a sense of being part of a unit, and gave them a deep sense of loyalty to the "buddies" who shared the hardships of military life with them. One midwesterner who was

Students studying in diesel lab at submarine training school, New London, Connecticut, August 1943
(National Archives)

sent to Georgia for his basic training and then fought in Germany recalled of his early weeks in the army:

> The first time I ever heard a New England accent was at Fort Benning. The southerner was an exotic creature to me . . . You had an incredible mixture of every stratum of society. And you're of that age when your need for friendship is greatest . . . There's a special sense of kinship. The reason you storm the beaches is not patriotism or bravery. It's that sense of not wanting to fail your buddies.

Part of every soldier's training consisted of presentations on U.S. war aims. The War Department produced a series of films called *Why We Fight,* which used documentary newsreel footage to explain the background and issues of the war. Many of the soldiers paid little attention to these lectures and films. Exhausted from their physical training, some fell asleep as soon as the lights were turned out to show training films of any kind.

It was not that the GIs were unpatriotic or cynical. But they had little in common with the flag-waving image of the American soldier offered in all too many war-era Hollywood movies. The favorite GI song was not a patriotic hymn like "God Bless America" or even a snappy ditty like the briefly popular "You're a Sap, Mister Jap." Instead, the most popular song was the sentimental, nostalgic tune "White Christmas" ("I'm dreaming of a White Christmas/With ev'ry Christmas card I write"). "White Christmas," first crooned by Bing Crosby in a 1942 film, was soon echoed in the rough voices of marines and GIs from the jungles of the South Pacific to the deserts of North Africa. As a marine veteran of the Peleliu and Okinawa campaigns in the South Pacific later recalled:

> There was nothing macho about the war at all. We were a bunch of scared kids who had to do a job. People tell me I don't act like an ex-marine. How is an ex-marine supposed to act? They have some Hollywood stereotype in mind. No, I don't look like John Wayne. We were in it to get it over with, so we could go back home and do what we wanted to do with our lives.

As the war continued, the American army became an increasingly effective fighting force. Yet it never completely lost its amateur quality.

Most American soldiers were soldiers only for the duration of the war. When victory came, they intended to shed their uniforms as quickly as possible. It was easy to tell the difference between the post-1940 draftees and the Regular Army soldiers who had joined up before the war began. The draftees never showed much concern with the spit-and-polish traditions of the professionals. Their uniforms were usually a mess. Their salutes and parade ground appearance fell far short of the military ideal.

When they went overseas, their lack of professionalism became even more apparent. European soldiers and even civilians were struck by the sloppiness of the American troops. Even when they marched in step, they never achieved the precise uniform motion required by most European armies, especially the Germans. Some laughed at the ragged look of the American GIs; others were impressed. A civilian in Czecho-slovakia told an American officer that when he saw American soldiers marching, he thought, "They walk like free men."

6

THE BIG THREE

At first glance, the aims of the United States in World War II appeared very simple: to win a military victory over the nation's enemies in Europe and the Pacific. But what would follow the Axis surrender? What kind of world did the United States want its victory to lead to? What role would the nation play in the postwar international order? Was there any way to guarantee that, 20 years after the end of the Second World War, America would not have to fight in still another world war? Who would be America's friends and who—if anyone—would be its enemy once Nazi Germany, Fascist Italy, and imperial Japan were defeated? These questions did not prove easy to answer.

In 1942, America's vision of the postwar world was still cloudy. But it was clear by then that Americans wanted to avoid any return to the international situation that followed World War I. During the First World War President Woodrow Wilson had called for a new kind of world order, where the United States would help guard against the outbreak of future wars as a member of the League of Nations. This was rejected by the U.S. Senate in 1919 and by American voters in 1920, when the Democrats were swept out of the White House. In the years that followed, the United States rejected the idea of "collective security" that the League of Nations imperfectly symbolized. With the coming of World War II, however, many Americans accepted that their government's isolationist policies had created the climate in which Axis aggression had flourished in the 1930s.

"We have profited by our past mistakes," President Roosevelt declared in 1942. "This time we shall know how to make full use of victory." He drew several lessons from the outcome of the First World War.

THE BIG THREE

First, Hitler's opponents should not settle for a partial victory. Germany had not been invaded during the First World War. Its armies, although battered, had simply withdrawn from France rather than surrender to the Allies after an armistice was agreed to in November 1918. That allowed the Nazis to benefit from the "stab-in-the-back" legend in the 1920s. This time it would be different. The aggressors would be taught the price of aggression. Roosevelt announced early in 1943 that the Allies were prepared to fight on until they had gained the "unconditional surrender" of the Axis powers.

Second, Roosevelt believed that the principle of national self-determination should be used to redraw the map of the postwar world. This meant that the peoples of all nations should be free to choose for themselves what kind of government they wanted to live under. In the First World War, Britain, France, and czarist Russia had drawn up a series of secret treaties that divided among themselves shares of enemy territory. When the United States joined the Allies in 1917, President Wilson had spoken idealistically for the right of self-determination. His ideas had little influence over the actual peace settlement. This time, Roosevelt believed, there should be no secret deals among the victors to carve up other nations' lands.

Finally, the president insisted, there must be no return to isolationism. The League of Nations had collapsed. But when victory came this time, there should be a new international organization to take its place, dedicated to maintaining the collective security of all nations. When this organization was established, the United States should become a leading force within it.

The United States was not fighting the war alone, and it was not up to Roosevelt alone to decide what kind of world a victory would lead to. Much would depend upon the attitude of U.S. allies,

Roosevelt with his trademark cigarette holder (Library of Congress)

British prime minister Winston Churchill *(Library of Congress)*

especially Great Britain and the Soviet Union. Although many other nations joined the coalition against the Axis powers, the United States, Britain, and the Soviet Union were the most powerful. They became known as the "Big Three."

Britain was America's closest ally, and Roosevelt developed close personal ties with the British prime minister, Winston Churchill. They met for the first time on a British warship, the *Prince of Wales,* anchored off Newfoundland in August 1941. Although the United States was not yet officially at war, the two leaders drew up a statement of common war aims. The most important of these, as outlined in Roosevelt and Churchill's Atlantic Charter, was the principle of self-determination. The United States and Great Britain would "respect the right of all peoples to choose the form of government under which they will live." The two countries would guarantee the restoration of "sovereign rights and self-government . . . to those who have been forcibly deprived of them."

Those were brave words at a time when Hitler's armies occupied most of the European continent. Such words also concealed differences within the Anglo-American alliance. Britain had its own empire, which controlled the lives of millions of people around the world who did not enjoy anything like a right of self-determination. Churchill understood the Atlantic Charter to apply only to the nations conquered by Hitler. Roosevelt wanted it to apply also to colonies around the world, including those controlled by wartime allies like Britain.

Britain and the United States also disagreed on military strategy. After Pearl Harbor Churchill came to Washington for a conference with Roosevelt. The two leaders confirmed their commitment to a "Europe First" policy. This meant that the United States and Britain would pour most of their energy and resources into the war against Hitler. They would turn their full attention to the war against Japan only after victory in Europe.

British and American armies would share more or less equally in the fighting in Europe, while the United States played the main role in the Pacific.

The United States and Britain were not able to resolve other strategic questions so easily. American generals favored the earliest possible return to the European continent, through an invasion of France across the English Channel. Churchill remembered the terrible losses of British manpower in the trenches of France in World War I. He advocated an alternative strategy of attacking what he called Europe's "soft under-belly." That meant staying out of France for as long as possible, concentrating instead on operations in the Mediterranean—in North Africa, Sicily, Italy, and Greece. These differences were never fully resolved. The actual strategy Britain and the United States would follow represented a compromise between the two.

The tensions that existed between the two English-speaking allies were minor compared to those that troubled the relations between the United States and Britain on the one hand, and their Big Three partner, the Soviet Union, on the other. There was a lot of mistrust that had to be overcome. The Atlantic Charter did not impress the Soviets. They remembered how in 1918 and 1919 both the United States and Britain had sent troops into Russia in a failed attempt to crush the Bolshevik Revolution. This violated Wilson's supposed commitment to self-determination. Why should they trust the West's words now?

For their part, the United States and Great Britain had not forgotten Soviet attempts to spread the doctrine of world revolution in the 1920s and 1930s. The tyrannical rule that Soviet leader Joseph Stalin maintained over his own people had done much to discredit the Soviet experiment in Western eyes. Stalin and Hitler had signed the Nazi-Soviet Pact in 1939, an agreement that gave Hitler a free hand in Poland and led directly to the start of the war. Many people had decided that the two dictators represented equally evil systems. This attitude did not change overnight when the Nazis invaded the Soviet Union of June 22, 1941. A common reaction in the United States was expressed by Missouri senator Harry Truman on June 23: "If we see that Germany is winning we ought to help Russia and if Russia is winning we ought to help Germany and that way let them kill as many as possible."

But Roosevelt and Churchill felt differently. If Hitler defeated the Soviet Union, he would gain unshakeable mastery of the European continent. At a news conference on June 24, Roosevelt pledged to send "all the aid we possibly can to Russia." Starting that October the United

States extended lend-lease aid to the Soviet Union. Due to delays in production and losses to German U-boats, however, significant military supplies did not reach the USSR until 1943.

In January 1941 Roosevelt had given a speech to Congress calling for a world reorganized around what he called the "Four Freedoms": freedom of speech, freedom of religion, freedom from fear, and freedom from want, or economic hardship. It would take a remarkable turnabout in public opinion to make most Americans accept the contradiction of fighting a war for freedom in alliance with a country that knew little freedom of any kind. The turnabout began after the Red Army's stubborn defense of Moscow in December 1941. Hitler's generals met their first serious military setback of the war. This won the admiration of many Americans. Then came the great Soviet victory at the battle of Stalingrad in early 1943, which would prove to be the turning point in the war against Hitler. This reinforced the belief that a country that fought so hard against the common enemy could not be so bad.

Americans were encouraged to forget about the repressive history of the Soviet regime. Stalin became "Uncle Joe" in U.S. news reports, and his portrait graced the covers of the leading American newsweekly magazines. *Life* magazine devoted a special issue to the Soviet Union shortly after the victory at Stalingrad. It paid the Russians the compliment of describing them as "one hell of a people [who] look like Americans, dress like Americans and think like Americans."

Secretary-General of the Communist Party of Soviet Russia, Joseph Stalin *(Library of Congress)*

Roosevelt had his first wartime meeting with Stalin in the Iranian capital, Tehran, late in 1943. When he returned he reported on the radio to Americans that "I got along fine with Marshal Stalin. I believe that we are going to get along very well with him and the Russian people—very well indeed." Behind the scenes, however, not everything was going so smoothly. There was no question that the United States and Britain needed Soviet help to defeat the Nazis. They could not run the risk

Battle of Stalingrad
TURNING POINT IN EUROPE

THE SOVIET UNION'S RED ARMY FOUGHT A DECISIVE battle in the war against Nazi Germany in the fall and winter of 1942–43. In the summer of 1942 Hitler had ordered his forces to seize the city of Stalingrad, an industrial center strategically located on the Volga River. At first the Germans made rapid progress, but when they fought their way into the city they met unexpectedly determined resistance from the Soviet defenders. The battle raged street by street, and even room by room in the city's battered buildings. In November the Red Army launched a counterattack, encircling the German Sixth Army, with its 270,000 men. Suffering terribly in the Russian winter from lack of warm clothing, food, and ammunition, the Germans fought on, but on February 2, 1943, the survivors were forced to surrender. After Stalingrad, the Nazis never again launched an offensive on the eastern front; they began a retreat that ended in Berlin in May 1945.

of Stalin signing another separate peace with Hitler, as he had done once before, in 1939. Roosevelt also believed that, if there was to be any chance for the achievement of a permanent peace, the western democracies must find a way to cooperate with the Soviet Union.

How could Roosevelt convince the deeply suspicious Soviet leader of his goodwill? Words were not enough, nor was lend-lease aid enough. While the Americans spent dollars, the Soviets were spending the blood of their people, 27 million of whom would die before the war ended. Stalin demanded that the Western allies launch a "second front" in western Europe as soon as possible to take some of the pressure off the hard-pressed Red Army. That was something that Roosevelt could not do, because of British reluctance and American military unpreparedness. What else could he give?

Stalin too was determined to avoid the mistakes of the past. Twice so far in the 20th century Russia had been invaded by Germany. The lesson he drew from history was that the Soviet Union, in order to defend itself, had to move its own borders westward. Russia would then protect those borders with a barrier of friendly states. That meant taking some of Poland's territory and holding on to Estonia, Latvia,

Three German soldiers walk down a desolate street in the ruins of Stalingrad, in the Soviet Union, September 1942. *(Library of Congress)*

and Lithuania (which had been annexed by the Russians during the period of the Nazi-Soviet Pact). It also meant installing a pro-Soviet government in Poland and perhaps in other countries in eastern Europe as well.

Stalin's goals could not be squared with the principles laid out in the Atlantic Charter. But the Red Army was moving steadily westward after the battle of Stalingrad, and the Western allies were unable to launch their second front invasion until well into 1944. There was not much that Roosevelt could do about it. All that he could hope to do was to postpone the inevitable uproar when Americans learned of Soviet intentions in eastern Europe. Publicly, Roosevelt continued to speak in terms of a peace shaped by self-determination. Privately, he reassured Stalin that the United States respected the Soviet desire for pro-Soviet governments along its border. Roosevelt was motivated by the desire to have nothing interfere with the spirit of wartime unity among the anti-Hitler coalition. Despite his best intentions, the seeds of the postwar cold war between the Western powers and the Soviet bloc were already being sown in the midst of the Big Three's war against Hitler.

7

THE TIDE TURNS
IN THE PACIFIC

From December 1941 through May 1942, Americans and their allies were forced to absorb a steady drumbeat of defeat in the Pacific: Pearl Harbor was bombed December 7; Guam fell December 10; that same day, the British battleships *Prince of Wales* and *Repulse* were sunk by Japanese planes in the South China Sea; the American garrison on Wake Island surrendered December 23; Δthe British garrison at Hong Kong surrendered on Christmas Day; the Japanese captured the port of Rabaul on the island of New Britain, along with other islands in the Solomon chain, in January 1942; all of Malaya, including Singapore, stronghold of British power in Southeast Asia, fell by mid-February; the Dutch East Indies, including the islands of Sumatra, Borneo, Celebes, and Java, fell in March; that same month, the Japanese scored a major naval victory in the nighttime battle of the Java Sea, destroying 12 Allied ships, including an American cruiser and destroyer; by mid-May the British army was driven out of Burma.

But the "rising sun" of Japanese empire had already reached the limit of its power in the spring of 1942. Few would have predicted this after such an unbroken string of Japanese military triumphs. Allied strategists feared the loss of Australia, New Zealand, Ceylon, even India to the Japanese. They had nightmares about the prospect of the Germans pushing eastward, through the Middle East and the Soviet Union, to link up with the Japanese pushing westward in India and China. The Axis powers would then be dominant on the entire Eurasian landmass.

WORLD WAR II

Americans were dismayed and angered by events in the Pacific. Roosevelt had agreed to a "Europe first" strategy for the war. Undoubtedly, if the choice had been up to the American public in 1942, they would have voted for a "Pacific first" onslaught against Japan. The war against Germany was accepted as a grim necessity, but aroused relatively little popular enthusiasm. The war against Japan, on the other hand, was a war for revenge. It meant revenge for the "sneak attack" on Pearl Harbor, for the humiliating American defeats that followed, for the mistreatment of American servicemen captured in battle. Among many Americans, the Pacific war aroused a real hatred for "the Japs."

During much of the winter and spring of 1942, the attention of Americans focused on the plight of the embattled defenders of Bataan and Corregidor in the Philippines. The American fleet was in no condition to come to their rescue. The only real question was how long MacArthur's soldiers could hold out until the inevitable defeat. As the symbol of American resistance in the Philippines, Gen. Douglas MacArthur became known as the "Lion of Luzon." His exploits were celebrated in press releases put out by his own staff and reprinted by reporters hungry for stories of American heroism. To his troops on Bataan, he was known by a less flattering nickname, "Dugout Doug," because he was so rarely seen outside of the deep fortifications built into Corregidor. Back in Washington Gen. Dwight D. Eisenhower, who had served under MacArthur in the Philippines in the late 1930s, confided his own doubts about the Lion of Luzon to his diary: "The public has built itself a hero out of its own imagination."

After securing Manila, the Japanese attacked the Bataan peninsula on January 9. Americans and Filipinos were driven back from their original lines to a new position midway down the peninsula. There they dug in and beat back the Japanese. In late January Gen. Masaharu Homma, Japanese commander in the

Gen. Douglas MacArthur
(Library of Congress)

American POWs at the Hands of the Germans and the Japanese

THE GENEVA CONVENTION OF 1929 CALLED FOR THE humane treatment of prisoners of war (POWs) in any future international conflicts. Germany was among the countries that ratified the agreement; Japan was not. During World War II, the Nazis selectively honored the Geneva rules. Soviet prisoners were treated with great brutality and died by the millions. But with American and British prisoners, the Germans were generally more lenient. 93,941 Americans were taken prisoner by the Germans during World War II. A few American captives were sent to gruesome concentration camps. But most were sent to POW camps, where the treatment was at least minimally humane. As a result, only 1 percent of American POWs in Europe died in captivity.

Americans taken prisoner by the Japanese were not so fortunate. Prisoners suffered from harsh treatment, scanty rations, poor sanitation, lack of medical treatment, and overwork. Of the 25,600 American POWs held by the Japanese during World War II, 45 percent died in captivity.

Philippines, withdrew his troops to refit and reinforce them. During this lull in the fighting, MacArthur received orders from Washington to leave for safety in Australia. Upon his arrival there on March 17, he declared, "I came through and I shall return." For the American public, MacArthur's return to the Philippines became one of the most eagerly awaited events of the war.

Gen. Jonathan Wainwright was left in command on Bataan, although MacArthur continued to send him orders from Australia. Among the last of these was a totally unrealistic directive for U.S. and Filipino forces to counterattack in April at the very moment their own defenses were crumbling. Although their bravery was celebrated at home, the soldiers on Bataan felt abandoned, as they expressed in a bitter song: "We're the Battling Bastards of Bataan/No mama, no papa, no Uncle Sam!" By the end of the battle, they were living on only a quarter of the normal food ration and were suffering the effects of malnutrition and tropical diseases. The Japanese resumed their offensive on April 3, and this time broke through the lines of weakened defenders. Bataan surrendered on April 9. General Wainwright, after making his way to

A captured Japanese photograph shows Japanese troops on Bataan, Philippines, in 1941. *(National Archives)*

Corregidor, continued to hold out on the fortified island with 13,000 defenders, until May 7.

Following Bataan's surrender, the Japanese marched their 75,000 prisoners some 55 miles to the railroad that would carry them to a prisoner-of-war camp. This became notorious as the "Bataan Death March," and after the war General Homma was tried and executed by the Allies for his role in it. Most of the prisoners were already weakened by months of too little to eat. They received little or no food and water along the march route. Stragglers were shot or bayoneted. By the time the march reached the railroad, some 600 Americans and more than 5,000 Filipinos had died. The death march was the product of Japanese miscalculation as well as brutality. They had expected to take only a third as many prisoners as they actually found on Bataan and did not have enough food for them all. By the standards of the

Japanese army, Homma was a relatively humanitarian commander. In fact, he would eventually be removed from his command in the Philippines by his military superiors for being "too soft." But private Japanese soldiers and some Japanese officers treated their captives with sadistic contempt. Japanese soldiers were taught to fight to the death. They looked down on as subhuman those who accepted the dishonor of surrender.

For Americans, the first bright spot in the news from the Pacific came on April 18. Sixteen B-25 bombers commanded by Lt. Col. James Doolittle bombed the Japanese capital of Tokyo. Doolittle's men took off from the carrier USS *Hornet* in a risky maneuver in high seas. They did not have enough fuel to make it back to the carrier. Instead, they were to fly to a Chinese airfield after completing the mission. But their planes ran out of fuel and they had to crash-land in China. Most of the pilots survived and eventually made their way back to the United States. The raid was of little military value, but it provided a morale boost for Americans. It also caused the Japanese to reconsider their

Prisoners with their hands tied behind their backs photographed during the Bataan Death March. *(National Archives)*

position in the central Pacific. This led to a fateful decision to try to capture the American base at Midway Island.

In the spring of 1942 the structure of the American military command in the Pacific was reorganized. Adm. Chester W. Nimitz was appointed commander of the Pacific fleet. The Pacific was divided into two theaters of operation. Nimitz took command of the Pacific Ocean Zone (the north and central Pacific). MacArthur was given command in the Southwest Pacific (Australia, New Guinea, the Bismarcks, and the Solomons). In addition, later in the year, Adm. William F. "Bull" Halsey was placed in command of naval forces in the Southwest Pacific region. The navy, the marines, the army, and the army air corps were now all involved in planning and carrying out combined land and sea operations. So the Pacific was not only divided into two separate zones, but each zone also had a commander from a different branch of the armed forces. Confusion and competition were inevitable. MacArthur and Nimitz fought a constant battle for control of troops and resources in the Pacific. In overall strategy, MacArthur sought to win control of New Guinea and the Solomons as stepping stones back to the Philippines. Nimitz—backed by the naval commander in chief in Washington, Adm. Ernest King—advocated "island-hopping" across the Pacific. This called for bypassing some of MacArthur's islands to gain air and naval bases from which Japan itself could someday be attacked.

One of the key developments in the war took place far from the battlefield in the spring of 1942. U.S. Navy codebreakers learned how to decipher the Japanese naval code—that is, they learned how to read the messages the Japanese believed were sent in a secret code. This gave a great advantage to American naval commanders, who could now anticipate their enemy's moves in the Pacific. The first time they were able to put this knowledge to work was in the Battle of the Coral Sea in May 1942. The Japanese had decided to capture Port Moresby on the southeast coast of New Guinea. They assembled a large force of carriers and heavy cruisers to provide cover for an invasion force. Nimitz, learning of Japanese intentions, assembled his own task force, including the carriers *Yorktown* and *Lexington*.

The initial contact between the two fleets came on May 4, with the main battle on May 7 and 8. It was the first major naval battle, anywhere, in which the ships involved never actually saw one another. The big guns on the Japanese and American battleships and cruisers were never fired, because the opposing fleets were miles out of each other's range. It soon became clear that the naval war in the Pacific would be a war of carriers and air power. The American loss of eight battleships at Pearl Harbor proved far less decisive than anyone would have believed on December 7.

The Battle of the Coral Sea was a confusing affair, as naval air battles tended to be. Reconnaissance pilots mistook oilers and destroyers for carriers and cruisers. Pilots on both sides reported sinking more and larger enemy ships than they had actually attacked. At one point American B-17s dropped their bombs on the American fleet (fortunately missing their target). On another occasion, as darkness and bad weather set in, several Japanese pilots attempted to land on an American carrier. They thought it was one of their own, but were shot down at the very moment safety seemed at hand.

Nor was the outcome of the battle clear. The Americans sank one small Japanese carrier and badly damaged a heavy cruiser. They also shot down a large number of Japanese planes. In turn the Japanese sank one of the precious U.S. carriers, the *Lexington,* and damaged another, the *Yorktown.* But if the ship tonnage lost was about equal, there was no question that the Coral Sea encounter was a strategic defeat for the Japanese. They were forced to abandon their attempt to attack Port Moresby from the sea. It was the first time in the war that a Japanese invasion force did not succeed in taking its objective.

Beginning in mid-May, navy cryptoanalysts (codebreakers) began to decipher messages indicating a Japanese plan to invade Midway Island. A Japanese invasion force under the command of Admiral Yamamoto, the architect of the Pearl Harbor attack, sailed in late May. It included four carriers, as well as battleships, cruisers, destroyers, and troop transports. Yamamoto also ordered the invasion of two Aleutian atolls, off the coast of Alaska. The plan was to draw American forces away from the central Pacific. Knowing that the main attack was set for Midway, Admiral Nimitz refused to be diverted northward. He prepared to meet the Japanese with the carriers *Enterprise, Hornet,* and *Yorktown.* This last one had been repaired with breakneck speed, at Pearl Harbor, from the damage it had suffered in the Coral Sea.

The Battle of Midway began on June 3, when reconnaissance flights from Midway detected the approach of the Japanese fleet. Bombers set off from Midway to attack the Japanese carriers but had no success. (Throughout the war, land-based bombers proved largely unable to hit naval targets.) June 4 was the critical day in the battle. In the morning

Japanese bombers attacked Midway, suffering heavy losses in the attack. The Japanese carrier commanders were unaware for several crucial hours of the presence of American carriers in the vicinity. They thus failed to protect themselves adequately. The Japanese, however, did successfully turn back several waves of land-based bombers and carrier-based torpedo planes, taking a heavy toll on the attackers. One squadron of torpedo planes from the *Hornet* lost all 16 of its planes, with only one man surviving. An American pilot recalled that the air above the carriers was "just like a beehive" with American torpedo planes, bombers, and fighters scrapping with Japanese fighters (the famed Zeros) and dodging antiaircraft fire, or "flak."

But the Japanese grew overconfident and made the mistake of keeping all their fighters at low altitude. The fighters were assigned to guard against American torpedo planes, which had to make a long, low, sweeping approach to launch their torpedoes. The Japanese were thus caught unprepared when U.S. dive-bombers from the *Enterprise* and *Yorktown* arrived on the scene. Within five minutes, three Japanese carriers were fatally damaged, as American bombs set off bombs and torpedoes piled up on their flight decks. The remaining, undamaged Japanese carrier launched its own air strike, which crippled the unlucky

A "beehive" of flak over the Battle of Midway *(Library of Congress)*

Yorktown. (The carrier was finished off on June 7 by a Japanese submarine.) Planes from the *Enterprise* and the *Hornet* revenged the *Yorktown* by hitting Yamamoto's last carrier. The four damaged Japanese carriers were little more than burning hulks, and all of them sank or were scuttled by their crews the next day.

The Battle of Midway proved to be a turning point in the war, although the battle might easily have gone the other way. Its outcome was the product of Japanese overconfidence as well as superior American intelligence gathering. Without the intercepted and decoded Japanese messages, Nimitz would not have known to concentrate his forces at Midway. The battle and the island might well have been lost. That would have posed a Japanese threat to Hawaii, which might have drawn American resources away from Europe. This might have delayed victory in both theaters of war for many years. After Midway the Japanese lost the initiative in the Pacific. They could strike no more knockout blows. From this point on it became a war of attrition—a gradual wearing down of the enemy's ability to resist. This was a war the Americans, with vastly greater resources at their disposal, seemed destined to win.

8

THE BATTLE OF
THE ATLANTIC

As the naval battles in the Pacific reversed the Japanese advance, another type of naval warfare was occurring in the Atlantic. This was the U-boat war, so named after the German word for a submarine, *Unterseeboot* (undersea boat). Both naval wars remind us that fighting a truly "world" war presented special challenges to the United States.

This was an era before long-range transport aircraft could easily cross the Atlantic. As a result, virtually every American soldier, gun, and bullet thrown into the battle against the Axis powers had to be transported thousands of miles by ship, in journeys that took days or even weeks. The United States was shipping and supplying not only its own troops. It also had to transport millions of tons of lend-lease supplies to its allies. The Germans had no intention of allowing this massive supply effort to flow smoothly. For the Allies to win the war in Europe, they first had to win the Battle of the Atlantic.

Hitler's concept of war was land-based, perhaps reflecting his experience as a foot soldier in World War I. He took a direct (although not always helpful) role in shaping the army's strategy, and he poured German resources into his *Wehrmacht* (army). Another top Nazi leader, Hermann Goering, had been a flying ace in the First World War. As air marshal, Goering oversaw the rebuilding of the *Luftwaffe* (air force). Germany's navy was the orphan among the nation's military services. Its rebuilding was low on the list of Nazi priorities during the 1930s. In the First World War, German U-boats had sunk more than 5,000 Allied ships. Yet submarine warfare did not figure into Hitler's ideas of how he would defeat his enemies in 1939. At the start of the war, the German navy had only 22 U-boats in service that were suitable for deep-water operations.

Adm. Karl Doenitz was a veteran of the U-boat campaign in World War I. As commander of the German navy's submarine service in 1939, he was determined to prove the value of his vessels to Germany's war effort. Less than 10 hours after Britain declared war on Germany on September 3, 1939, a U-boat had sunk its first victim, the British passenger liner *Athenia*. It had been heading for the United States, and 28 Americans were among the 140 passengers who lost their lives.

Hitler had initially hoped to negotiate a settlement with Britain to end the war, so he was upset by the sinking of the *Athenia*. But even before the first month of the war was over, he had begun to lift restrictions on U-boat operations. By the end of 1939, Doenitz's U-boats had sunk 215 merchant ships, along with a British aircraft carrier and battleship. The war in the Atlantic, unlike that on the western front in 1939, was never a "phony war." From the very beginning it was a desperate struggle to kill or be killed.

The British were unwilling to talk peace even after being driven from the European continent in the spring of 1940. Hitler became more sympathetic to Doenitz's arguments that the way to defeat Britain was to starve it into submission. From the start of the war Britain had been dependent on imports of food, wool, lumber, rubber, iron ore, and oil transported by sea from the Commonwealth countries and from neutral trading partners like the United States. British leaders remembered all too clearly how close the Germans had come in World War I to shutting down their vital supply links across the Atlantic. "The only thing that ever really frightened me," Churchill would write after the war, "was the U-boat peril."

The German U-boat fleet proved its value from the outset of the war. Yet from 1939 through most of 1941 Hitler was slow to shift Germany's industrial resources into the production of new submarines. Germany also used "pocket battleships" (so called for their relatively small size) like the *Admiral Graf Spee* and regular battleships like the *Bismarck* for surface raids against British merchant ships and Royal Navy vessels.

In December 1939 the crew of the *Graf Spee* scuttled their ship after being forced by the Royal Navy to take shelter in a Uruguayan port. In

May 1941 the Royal Navy sank the supposedly unsinkable *Bismarck.* Hitler changed his strategy. He kept his remaining surface vessels in protective shelter for much of the rest of the war, and allowed an enormous expansion of U-boat production. By August 1942 Doenitz had more than 300 submarines under his command. The new U-boats were wider-ranging and deeper-diving than earlier models.

With Germany's blitzkrieg victories of spring 1940, Doenitz gained new ports in Norway and France for his U-boat fleet. This greatly lengthened the amount of time the submarines could spend on patrol in the Atlantic. What German submariners came to call the "Happy Time" was about to begin. U-boats sank 56 ships in August, 59 in September, and 63 in October 1940. German airplanes and surface raiders sank dozens more.

The British had to give up bringing ships into their southwestern ports, the ones closest to the U-boats' home bases. Instead, the western ports of Liverpool and Glasgow became Britain's link with the outside world. During the "Happy Time" each one of Doenitz's U-boats sank a monthly average of eight Allied vessels. Bad weather and the need to bring his ships in for repair and maintenance led Doenitz to curtail the campaign in the winter of 1940. In the spring of 1941, however, they were back to their deadly work.

To counter the success of the U-boat campaign, the British soon reintroduced the convoy system used in World War I. Rather than allowing each merchant vessel to take its chances in U-boat-infested waters, the British would gather together large numbers of ships and shepherd them to friendly ports. Such convoys were accompanied by destroyers and other Royal Navy vessels. The convoy defenders were equipped with sonar, a transmitting device that sent out a sound wave. This produced a distinctive "ping" when it bounced off a submerged object. The "pings" could be tracked on a screen to reveal the location of submarines. The destroyers could then move in with depth charges (barrels of high explosive programmed to go off when they were dropped to a set depth) to destroy the U-boats. Sonar was not totally reliable, especially in the version used in the early years of the war. It was of no use in detecting surface vessels. Submarines, despite their names, often attacked at night from the surface, using their deck gun to blow holes in the hulls of merchant ships.

In the spring of 1941, the British introduced another technological innovation, planes and ships equipped with radar (a word made up

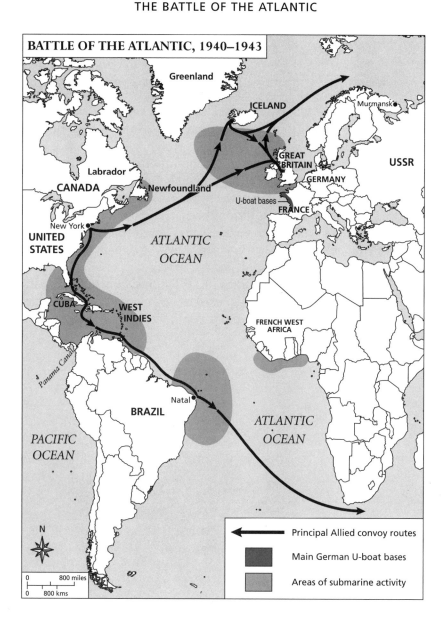

BATTLE OF THE ATLANTIC, 1940–1943

from *r*adio *d*etecting *a*nd *r*anging). This recently developed technology could reveal the presence of surface ships from many miles away. Again, it would take several years before the radar equipment and techniques were perfected. Doenitz responded to improvements in convoy defenses with "wolf pack" tactics in which U-boats would group together to trail and harass the convoys.

America's first casualties in World War II were suffered in the undeclared naval war in the Atlantic in the fall of 1941. Then, when Germany declared war on the United States in December, Doenitz ordered an all-out assault on coastal shipping along the U.S. East Coast code-named Operation *Paukenschlag* ("Drum Roll").

When American ships sailed to Britain, they automatically joined convoys. At first, though, no one had thought it necessary to set up convoys for ships hugging the American coast. With no more than a dozen U-boats, Doenitz was able to bring the war as close as it would ever come to American mainland shores. Thirty-seven ships were sunk in American waters between January and May 1942, many of them oil tankers. The bright lights of America's coastal cities were still undimmed by any blackout orders. The lights silhouetted the dark shapes of the merchant ships that passed by and made them perfect targets for U-boats. The resort town of Miami, Florida, was still crowded

A merchant officer, his suitcase lowered to a waiting lifeboat, prepares to descend a Jacob's ladder and abandon his sinking ship. *(Library of Congress)*

with tourists in the winter of 1942. They would gather each night on the beach to watch the torpedoed ships burning and sinking.

U.S. Navy officers at first stubbornly ignored British advice on counter-submarine warfare. Instead they had to learn through their own bitter experience what two years of war had taught their ally. The Americans gradually learned about the necessity for convoys and the uselessness of sending out patrols to "hunt" randomly for U-boats over broad stretches of ocean. U.S. coastal blackouts were finally enforced in mid-May 1942. When convoys were introduced in the summer of 1942, they dramatically reduced coastal sinkings.

In 1942 Doenitz came close to winning the battle of the Atlantic. The Allies lost a million tons more shipping than they were able to replace with new shipping. The U-boats enjoyed their best month of the war that June, sinking 144 Allied ships. This was a return of the "Happy Time" for German submariners, but it was a very unhappy time for Allied strategists. They had already begun a massive buildup of personnel and materials in the British Isles. This was to be used for a cross-Channel invasion of France. If the Allies were unable to secure their Atlantic supply routes, the entire outcome of the war in western Europe was at risk.

The United States was also beginning to ship significant amounts of lend-lease aid to the Soviet Union. The "Murmansk run" from Iceland or Scotland past German-occupied Norway to the Soviet ports of Murmansk and Archangel was turning into a nightmare for merchant ships and their escort vessels. One convoy bound for Murmansk left Iceland on June 27, 1942, with 35 merchant ships, 22 of them American. Before they reached the Soviet Union, 24 of the ships had been sunk by German planes and U-boats. Four hundred thirty tanks and 210 aircraft intended for the hard-pressed Red Army and air force lay on the ocean floor.

Apart from some civilian victims of the Pearl Harbor bombing, the sailors of the merchant marine were virtually the only American civilians to be killed by enemy attack in the Second World War. In fact, through most of 1942 the U.S. Merchant Marine was suffering proportionately higher losses in men than any of the U.S. military services. No sailor shipping out of an Atlantic port in the first years of the war could assume he would ever return home. The deaths that awaited them if they were torpedoed in the North Atlantic were sure to be quick. In the freezing water of the Murmansk run, a man could not survive much more than 10 minutes.

The folksinger Woody Guthrie, composer of "This Land Is Your Land," served in the merchant marine during the war. He was twice aboard ships that were torpedoed. In June 1944 he was sailing on a troop carrier called the *Sea Porpoise*, carrying 3,000 soldiers bound for the Normandy front, when there was a U-boat alert. With the sound of depth charges echoing all around, he decided to go down into the ship's hold to conduct an impromptu concert for the soldiers. "Sing loud," he told the nervous soldiers, "it sends out shock waves that confuse the Nazi U-boats and makes 'em shoot crooked." Soon he had them singing and dancing to improvised square dance calls like "Grab your partner from his bunk/Whirl him around and show some spunk/Don't listen to the depth charge, just be brave/And we'll dance around old Hitler's grave."

When the tide in the battle of the Atlantic finally turned in the spring of 1943, it was as much a scientific and industrial victory as a military one. Radar-equipped long-range planes, based in Newfound-

Escort carrier planes drop bombs on a surfaced Nazi submarine somewhere in the Atlantic ocean. Germans run for cover as a bomb scores a near miss. *(National Archives)*

land, Iceland, and Northern Ireland, as well as planes launched from the U.S. Navy's new escort carriers, provided nearly continuous air cover for the convoys. The British had learned how to decipher the coded radio communications between U-boats, and were able to anticipate their moves. New weapons such as the Hedge Hog—a multiple-barreled mortar that shot 24 bombs at a time into the sea—began to replace the less efficient depth charges.

As a result of these changes, the number of Allied ships lost to the enemy dropped dramatically while U-boat losses steadily increased. Forty-one U-boats were sent to the bottom of the Atlantic in May 1943, one of them including Doenitz's son among its crew. Doenitz was forced to withdraw his fleet. Over the next year only 92 Allied ships were sunk in the Atlantic, fewer than the average monthly toll in 1942. At the same time, the number of ships available to the Allies for transport greatly increased. Liberty ships, which were cargo vessels built from prefabricated sections, rolled out of American shipyards at a rate of 140 a month in 1943. In the Atlantic, as in the Pacific, the Allies had been forced to hang on through a long series of defeats. The Nazis had failed to deliver the knockout blow in the battle of the Atlantic. With America's enormous industrial capacity now fully harnessed for the conflict, the eventual Allied victory seemed inevitable.

9
CARRYING THE WAR TO HITLER

When and where would the Allies strike back at Hitler? Allied political leaders and military strategists had decided on a "Europe first" policy even before American entry into the war. In the months after Pearl Harbor, they had to decide on exactly when and where the attack would come. The simplest answer, an invasion of France across the English Channel in 1942, was the one initially favored by American strategists. It was also favored by the Soviets. They hoped that a "second front" opened on Hitler's western flank would relieve the pressure their armies faced on the eastern front. The British, however, resisted this approach and stressed the dangers of a premature landing in France. The decision was eventually made to engage the Germans in a completely different theater, North Africa.

There was no doubt in Joseph Stalin's mind about what the United States and Great Britain should be doing in 1942. That was, start killing Germans as soon and on as massive a scale as possible. The western Allies' delay in establishing a second front provoked dark suspicions in the mind of the Soviet leader. What were they waiting for? Did they hope to see Nazi Germany and the Soviet Union bleed each other to death on the eastern front? Would they then step in militarily at the last moment and establish their own uncontested domination of Europe?

President Roosevelt was aware of Stalin's suspicions and eager to put them to rest. He had his own reasons for wanting to put American soldiers into battle with Hitler as soon as possible. Americans were already fighting and dying in the Pacific. Continued inactivity in Europe would

EUROPE, NOVEMBER 1942

■ Axis powers	1 1941–42 British and Axis forces battle across desert	7 December 5, 1941–April 1942 Russian counter- offensive
▨ Allied with Axis	2 April 6–17, 1941 German invasion of Yugoslavia	8 October 23–November 4, 1942 Battle of El Alamein
▨ Occupied by Germany	3 April 6–28, 1941 German invasion of Greece	9 November 8, 1942 Allied landings in North Africa
▨ Vichy French	4 May 20–29, 1941 Invasion of Crete	10 November 9, 1942 German landings in Tunisia
▨ Allied counter- offensives	5 June 22, 1941 Operation Barbarossa: Germany invades Russia	11 November 11, 1942 Germany occupies Vichy France
▨ Neutral powers	6 September 15, 1941 Leningrad besieged	12 November 19, 1942 Russian counter- offensive

only strengthen the demands of those who favored striking back at Japan with America's full military power. This would postpone the fight against Hitler indefinitely. American military leaders were also eager to test their troops against the Nazis. Their memories of the war in Europe in 1917 and 1918 were of smashing victories won at the cost of a relatively small number of American lives.

The British, however, had a very different perspective. Their memories of the First World War were of prolonged bloodletting in the trenches of the western front from 1914 through 1918. They had already grappled with the Germans in France during this second war, in the disaster-filled spring of 1940. It was not an experience they were eager to repeat. Finally, they knew that if any major continental invasion was to be launched in 1942 it would be made up primarily of British soldiers. The Americans were still training and outfitting their army. They could not possibly get across the Atlantic in large enough numbers to play much of a role.

For all these reasons, the British refused to go along with the idea of a 1942 invasion of France. Instead, they proposed that American and British forces land in the French colonies of North Africa. That would give them a base from which they could drive eastward against the Germans in Libya and Egypt. This would relieve the pressure on the British army in Egypt and secure the Mediterranean for Allied shipping. The invasion of North Africa could also serve as a rehearsal for the invasion of France.

The Americans reluctantly agreed. They did not think that Hitler could be defeated by this kind of sideshow operation. However, they had no practical alternative other than to go along. Churchill assured Roosevelt that he would travel to Moscow to bring the bad news to Stalin in August. Stalin swallowed his disappointment and to Churchill's surprise asked God's blessing on the North African venture. Any doubts remaining among the Americans about the wisdom of postponing the invasion of France were dispelled by the example of the Dieppe raid.

On the night of August 18, 1942, a force of 6,000 Allied troops (mostly Canadian but including a small unit of American Rangers) sailed across the English Channel for a "reconnaissance in force" against the French port of Dieppe. The raiders were spotted by the Germans before they got near the shore. They ran into three times the number of German defenders they expected to find there. Although they fought their way ashore and blew up a German gun battery, casualties were heavy and withdrawal difficult. Fully half the raiding force was killed, wounded, or captured. Dieppe taught Allied strategists some valuable lessons. They abandoned their initial notion that the invasion should land at many spots along the French coast. Instead, they decided to apply overwhelming force in one central landing area, supported by a heavy naval and aerial bombardment. Hasty improvisation, they learned, was a recipe for disaster. The invasion would have to be planned down to the smallest detail to succeed. But the Germans also learned some lessons from Dieppe and began to build up their coastal defenses.

The British had been fighting a seesaw battle for control of the eastern half of North Africa since 1940. Benito Mussolini dreamed of matching Hitler's victories with glorious conquests of his own. There had been little glory for the Italians in entering the war against France at the last moment, in June 1940. The Italians simply snatched a little piece of French territory while the Germans did all the real fighting. In September 1940, acting on his own, Mussolini sent an invasion force eastward from the Italian colony of Libya. The plan was to seize Egypt and the Suez Canal. British troops stationed in Egypt pushed back the invasion, which turned into a rout for the Italians. The British took 130,000 prisoners at a cost of less than 2,000 casualties. They pursued the Italians deep into Libya, capturing the key port cities of Tobruk and Benghazi by February 1941.

But the British soon encountered a more formidable enemy in North Africa. Hitler stepped in to bail out his hapless ally Mussolini. In February 1941 Lt. Gen. Erwin Rommel arrived in Libya to take command of a force of German tanks and motorized infantry known as the Afrika Korps. Rommel had already proven his abilities as a tank commander in the invasion of France. He would become known as the Desert Fox for his skillful adaptation to the harsh conditions of desert fighting. Although reserved in his personal manner, he won the devotion of his troops and was admired even by his enemies.

One German general referred to North Africa as "a tactician's paradise and a quartermaster's hell." Indeed, the retreats and advances of the next year and a half of warfare depended greatly on which side was receiving the best supplies. The desert war was fought on a vast, featureless battlefield, where the ability to move tanks and troops rapidly decided the fate of campaigns. Everywhere the armies went they had to be followed by trucks carrying water, food, gasoline, and ammunition. Offensives repeatedly ground to a halt when armies outran those supplies.

Rommel's Afrika Korps attacked the British in the spring of 1941, driving them back into Egypt. A mixed force of British, Australian, and Indian troops was able to retain a toehold in Libya at the port of Tobruk. There they mounted an epic resistance to Rommel's siege. The

"The Desert Fox", Lt. Gen. Erwin Rommel, Commander of the Afrika Korps *(Library of Congress)*

British whose forces had been reorganized as the Eighth Army, returned to the offensive in November. They relieved the garrison at Tobruk on December 10. By January 1942 the British had driven the Afrika Korps almost as far back into Libya as they had the Italians the previous year. But it was too soon to count the Desert Fox out. His resupplied Afrika Korps hit back with a new offensive in May 1942. This time the Germans captured Tobruk and then thrust deeply into Egypt. For a time it looked as though Rommel would make it all the way to the Suez Canal. This would have been a terrible setback for the Allied cause. Hitler rewarded Rommel for his victories by promoting him to the rank of field marshal.

Britain's Eighth Army, meanwhile, received a new commander, Gen. Bernard "Monty" Montgomery. Arrogant and methodical in command, Monty's slowness in launching attacks would infuriate other Allied generals. But when he fought, he fought to win. Montgomery hit the Germans hard at the battle of El Alamein in October 1942, driving the outnumbered Afrika Korps back across Libya and into Tunisia. This time it was for good: The Germans were never again a threat in the eastern part of North Africa.

It was ironic that Montgomery won his smashing victory over Rommel before the Anglo-American invasion of the western shores of North Africa took place. This invasion was code-named Operation Torch, and aiding the beleaguered Eighth Army had been one of the chief justifications for the operation in its planning stages. From the start, the North African campaign proved full of surprises for the Allies, most of them less pleasant than the victory at El Alamein.

One of the stranger aspects of Operation Torch was that there were no Axis troops at all in French Morocco and Algeria, the two French colonies slated for invasion. Instead, the invaders would face 120,000 French troops stationed there, and no one knew for sure which side they were on. When the French armies surrendered in France in June 1940, Hitler agreed that his troops would occupy only the northern half of the country. The southern half of France would be spared, at least for the moment, the disgrace of foreign occupation. A new French government, headed by an aging World War I hero, Marshal Henri Pétain, was set up in the small city of Vichy in central France. It was allowed to rule on the condition that it collaborated fully with the Nazis.

Not all the French were willing to accept Vichy's rule. Some joined resistance movements in France. Others escaped from France to England to join the Free French forces, headed by Gen. Charles de Gaulle, and to fight on the side of the Allies. French colonies around the world were divided in their loyalties between Vichy and Free French supporters. In North Africa, pro-Vichy forces were in power. The Allies, however, thought they had secured an agreement to allow their landings to take place without interference.

Operation Torch began on November 8, 1942. Eighty-five thousand American and 23,000 British troops headed for shore at three separate locations in French Morocco and Algeria. (No landings took place in French Tunisia, because the beaches were thought to lie too near enemy air bases in Sicily.) The secret deals that were supposed to have smoothed the way for the Allied landings did not work out as expected. In Algeria the invaders ran into only light resistance. The Americans in Morocco, however, had to face three days of heavy resistance from French soldiers before local

Gen. Bernard Montgomery, commander of Britain's Eighth Army, on arrival in London after victorious Africa campaign *(National Archives)*

commanders agreed to a cease-fire. Meanwhile, the Germans responded to the invasion by sending their own troops into both southern France and Tunisia.

Dwight D. Eisenhower, an obscure American general with no previous combat experience, had been assigned overall command of the Anglo-American invasion force. Eisenhower's appointment turned out to be a shrewd move. The friendly, low-key "Ike" proved a master both in planning the logistics of a complicated invasion and in managing the strong-willed, jealous, and often egotistical Allied generals under his command. Not the least of his qualifications for command was a willingness to recognize problems in his own army that needed correcting.

Tunisia became the last bastion of Axis strength on the African continent, as Hitler rushed reinforcements to the Afrika Korps. British

Aerial view of a first landing on the coast of North Africa, November 1942 *(National Archives)*

forces under Eisenhower's command, along with elements of the U.S. First Infantry Division and First Armored Division, tried to push the Germans out of Tunisia. They made it as far as the mountainous western half of the country. By late December winter rains and heavy mud had ground the Allied offensive to a halt.

Even without the bad weather, the Americans would have been in trouble. These first weeks of American ground operations against the Nazis were revealing. On the whole, American troops were poorly trained and poorly handled by their officers. Some of the soldiers who landed on November 8 had been armed with weapons that they had never before fired and did not know how to load. American planes wound up strafing columns of American soldiers. Coordination between U.S. and British units was uncertain at best. Eisenhower admitted:

> The best way to describe our operations to date is that they have violated every recognized principle of war, are in conflict with all operational and logistic methods laid down in textbooks, and will be condemned in their entirety by all . . . [U.S. Army] War College classes for the next twenty-five years.

Unfortunately, these were not the kind of problems that could be corrected overnight. The Germans still had some bloody lessons to teach the Americans in Tunisia.

10

MEDITERRANEAN OFFENSIVE

North Africa and Sicily

In 1943 the Allied offensive against Hitler picked up momentum. It did so in the Mediterranean—in North Africa, Sicily, and Italy—a region that was not a priority to American military strategists. Every new campaign the Allies launched in the Mediterranean delayed further what U.S. Army Chief of Staff George C. Marshall called the "main show," the invasion of France. But the hard-fought battles of 1943 did prove invaluable in toughening the inexperienced U.S. Army. They brought new leaders to the fore and prepared common soldiers and officers alike for the day when they would finally come to grips with the main force of Hitler's military might.

Roosevelt and Churchill met nine times during the course of the war. The Casablanca conference of January 14–24, 1943, was their first meeting on Churchill's side of the Atlantic. This city in Morocco until recently had been controlled by Hitler's semi-ally, Vichy France. Stalin, the third partner of the Big three, had been invited to this meeting, but declined. He was not going to be happy with the decisions Churchill and Roosevelt made in Casablanca, because once again the second-front invasion of Europe would be postponed.

Before the Casablanca conference, U.S. Army leaders felt that all American resources sent to Europe should be concentrated in England in preparation for a cross-Channel invasion. But Germany's seizure of Tunisia undermined their arguments. The Allies would have a fight on

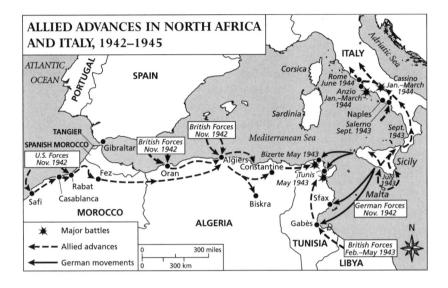

ALLIED ADVANCES IN NORTH AFRICA AND ITALY, 1942–1945

their hands for a good part of the coming year to drive the Germans completely out of North Africa. More American troops and supplies would have to be poured into the North Africa battle. This made it impractical to plan for an invasion of France anytime in 1943. The second front would have to wait until 1944. But after the Allies had driven the Germans from Tunisia, what would their armies do for the rest of 1943? They could not just sit around and let the Red Army do all the fighting against the Nazis. Roosevelt feared that if Stalin felt the Allies were not pulling their weight in the anti-Axis coalition, he might make a separate peace with Hitler.

If invading France was out of the question, where could they strike next? Churchill suggested an invasion of Sicily, the large island located off the tip of the Italian boot, only 100 sea miles from Tunisia. The conquest of Sicily would represent a stepping-stone back to the European continent and might lead to the crumbling of the increasingly unstable Fascist regime in Italy. Depending on their progress in Sicily, the Allies could then consider whether they would push on to the Italian mainland. The Americans were not enthusiastic about prospects for an Italian invasion, but they went along with the proposal to invade Sicily. Despite their intentions, the Americans found themselves steadily drawn into Churchill's Mediterranean strategy. General Marshall referred to it as the "suction pump" effect, with one successful invasion in the region leading to another.

Meanwhile, the Germans were going through their own debate over North African strategy. Hitler's decision to pour troops and supplies into Tunisia did not make Field Marshal Rommel happy. In his own mind he had already written off North Africa as an Allied victory. By mid-February 1943 the British had captured Tripoli and cleared the last of Rommel's rear guard from Libya. He wanted the German army withdrawn so that it could live to fight another day on a more promising battlefield. But Hitler would not listen and, as on other occasions during the war, a German army was thrown away due to his stubbornness.

Rommel, ordered to fight it out with the Allies in North Africa, took the offensive with an attack in mid-February against U.S. forces in western Tunisia. Rommel hoped to achieve a breakthrough to the Allied supply base at Tebessa, which was just across the border from Tunisia in Algeria. The American troops of U.S. II Corps, under the command of Gen. Lloyd Fredendall, were dug into a valley between two high mountain ranges in western Tunisia. Behind them lay the Kasserine Pass, which guarded the western approach to Tebessa. In front of them, to the east, lay the Faid Pass.

The Americans had heard from local Arabs that the Germans had some kind of monster tank, but they scoffed at the rumor. They soon

Tank war in the desert *(National Archives)*

discovered that the Arabs had not exaggerated. On Valentine's Day, February 14, 1943, new German Mark VI Tiger tanks, armed with 88 mm cannons, came roaring through the Faid Pass. The Americans' Sherman tanks were exposed to German fire well before the Tiger tanks came into range of the Shermans' weaker 75 mm guns. The effect was devastating. The Third Battalion of the U.S. First Armored Regiment lost 44 tanks the first day. The next day the Second Battalion lost 46 of its 50 tanks. By February 16, the Americans were in panicky retreat. All told, 192 Americans were killed, 2,624 were wounded, and 2,450 were captured in the battle of Kasserine Pass.

In the next few days the Germans drove 50 miles through the American lines. By February 22 American forward positions were a mere 12 miles from the Tebessa supply dumps. The Germans were halted just short of their objective by a mixed group of British and American troops. Using 105 mm cannon as antitank guns, they were finally able to stop the German panzers (tanks). The battle of Kasserine Pass, however, left the British worried about the fighting abilities of their American allies.

British generals wanted to keep the American units out of combat for the rest of the North African campaign. Eisenhower, as supreme commander, would not permit this. Instead he decided to shake up the command of the American armies. The unfortunate General Fredendall was sent back to the United States to take on a training assignment. A new general, George S. Patton, took his place as commander of II Corps. Patton, an experienced tank commander, was known for the bloodthirsty speeches he gave to his troops. Before long he began to be called "Old Blood-and-Guts" in the American press. Like MacArthur in the Pacific, Patton cut a dramatic figure. He was seldom seen in public without the two ivory-handled pistols he wore in his holsters. He was a spit-and-polish, hardfighting commander who instilled a new sense of discipline and self-confidence in the demoralized American troops.

While the Allies reorganized, the Germans' situation grew steadily worse. Allied planes and submarines were taking an increasing toll on Axis supply ships in the Mediterranean. The German tanks were running low on fuel and ammunition. Rommel's offensive had been a last-gasp effort; the Germans could not hold out much longer in North Africa. Montgomery, commander of the British Eighth Army, launched an assault on Tunisia's southeastern flank in mid-March, while Patton's revived II Corps pressed the attack from western Tunisia. The port cities of Tunis and Bizerte fell to the Allies on May 7. Final surrender

Experienced tank
commander "Old
Blood-and-Guts" Gen.
George S. Patton
(Library of Congress)

came on May 13, 1943. Rommel had already returned to Europe; most of
the Germans Hitler had sent in as final reinforcements were dead or had
been taken prisoner.

The U.S. forces had suffered 19,000 killed, wounded, captured, or missing since the initial landings in Morocco and Algeria in November 1942.
Total Allied casualties in the theater since 1940 amounted to 260,000 men.
The toll for the Axis powers was 620,000 casualties in the same period. By
driving the Germans and Italians completely out of North Africa, the
Allies had secured the Suez Canal and supplies of Middle East oil. In that
respect, they had won a great victory. But the campaign may have delayed
the coming of final victory in Europe by six months or longer. The Allies
had spent a half-year in North Africa accomplishing what was supposed to
be a quick mopping-up operation of a month or so.

MEDITERRANEAN OFFENSIVE

Long before victory was secured in Tunisia, planning had begun for the next step in the Mediterranean, the invasion of Sicily, code-named Operation Husky. The Allies assembled the largest amphibious invasion fleet in history, some 3,300 ships all told. In Sicily, the Axis powers had gathered a formidable force of 350,000 troops to defend the island. But the overwhelming majority of that force were from the Italian army, and their morale and loyalty to Mussolini's regime was rapidly crumbling. There were, however, 30,000 Germans among them, and Hitler sent in reinforcements after the invasion to bring their numbers up to 50,000. Sicily would not be a pushover.

The invasion began with a stroke of luck. Landing in bad weather in the early morning hours of July 10, the Allies caught the defenders off guard. But not everything went smoothly for the Allies, particularly for the paratroopers and glider-borne troops. They wound up scattered far from their assigned objectives and suffered heavy casualties. On the invasion beaches along the island's southern and eastern shores the Allies met with only light opposition from the Italian coastal defenders. Many of them deserted and shed their uniforms at the first opportunity. The Allies had put 150,000 ashore by the third day of the invasion,

Under a five-inch-bore cannon, a sailor looks out on the armada forming in a North African harbor for the invasion of Sicily. *(Library of Congress)*

securing their control of Sicily's southern coast, including the city of Syracuse. But as they moved north, they encountered German troops under the command of the highly capable Gen. Albrecht von Kesselring. The Sicilian campaign bogged down.

The original plan for the invasion was for the British Eighth Army under Montgomery to move up the eastern coast to capture the key northeastern port city of Messina, just a few miles by sea from the toe of the Italian boot. The U.S. Seventh Army under Patton was supposed to guard Montgomery's southern flank from counterattack. Montgomery moved his army at his customary deliberate pace, slowed even further by determined German resistance.

Patton soon became impatient with Montgomery's slow progress and his own subordinate role. He gained permission to send his troops heading along the opposite coast to Palermo, a port on Sicily's northwestern corner. The Americans made rapid progress against relatively light Italian resistance, and were welcomed into Palermo as liberators by jubilant crowds on July 22. The warm welcome the Allies received from the Sicilians was a good indication that Mussolini's days in power were numbered. The Fascist dictator had brought his subjects nothing but

Soldiers debark from landing barges at beachhead in Sicily, while antiaircraft guns are deployed to fend off Axis counterattacks.
(Library of Congress)

hardship and disaster. On July 25, two weeks after the start of the Sicilian invasion, Victor Emmanuel III, king of Italy, ordered Mussolini's arrest. This brought to an end the 21 years of his dictatorship. By the end of the month Mussolini's successor, Field Marshal Pietro Badoglio, was making secret overtures to the Allies to offer Italy's surrender. The Axis was beginning to crack.

Patton saw Sicily as an opportunity to wipe away all memory of the American disgrace at the Kasserine Pass. He no sooner reached Palermo than he shifted his attention to another prize. The British were still stalled in their drive for Messina. Patton's troops now set off across the northern coast of the island seeking to snatch the city before Montgomery's troops got there. "This is a horse race," Patton declared, "in which the prestige of the U.S. Army is at stake."

Patton's horse race was run on a dangerous obstacle course. The Germans proved themselves masters of defensive fighting in Sicily's mountainous terrain—a foretaste of things to come in Italy. American troops took heavy casualties as they fought their way hilltop to hilltop and village to village through Sicily's northern interior. Along the coastal road the Americans made a series of new amphibious landings in back of dug-in German units. The goal was to cut off the Germans, but the tactic had only mixed success. Progress proved slow and costly.

Patton was never the most patient of men. In early August, he let his frustration get the best of him and nearly destroyed his own career as a result. In two separate incidents while visiting U.S. military hospitals, he struck and swore at young soldiers suffering from combat fatigue. In the second incident he even drew one of his pearl-handled pistols, waved it in the soldier's face, and screamed, "You ought to be lined up against a wall and shot. In fact I ought to shoot you myself right now, goddamn you!"

Since the First World War combat fatigue, or "shell shock," had been recognized as a legitimate and serious psychological problem. The soldier Patton threatened with his pistol was no coward; he had performed bravely in combat in both Tunisia and Sicily until his nerves gave out. For an officer to strike an enlisted man, particularly one confined in a hospital, was a grave offense. It could have cost Patton his command. When news of the incident reached the United States, it created an uproar. Eisenhower, knowing how valuable a soldier Patton was, left him in command but required him to apologize to the two soldiers.

In the end, Patton's troops won their "horse race." An American patrol reached Messina on August 17. When British tanks showed up a few hours later, one of the Americans yelled to them "Where have you tourists been?" Sicily had been conquered. Twelve thousand Germans had been killed or wounded, 147,000 Italians surrendered, and the Allies lost 31,158 men killed, wounded, and missing. It would have been an even greater victory, had it not been for the successful German evacuation of a sizable portion of their army. Allied bombers were able to put some of the Axis boats out of commission, but 39,000 Germans escaped. The Allies would soon meet some of those same troops in Italy, as the Mediterranean offensive continued.

11

HARNESSING AMERICA'S ECONOMIC MIGHT

The Second World War was a total war. No single military battle or campaign on land or sea was going to decide the outcome of the war. The Allies and the Axis powers both understood the need to mobilize their home fronts so that they could outproduce, outshoot, and outlast their enemies. In the United States the war affected almost every aspect of life at home between 1941 and 1945. Industry, science, education, agriculture, transportation, journalism, and even the entertainment business enlisted for "the duration." U.S. industrial war production, in particular, was a major factor deciding the outcome of the war. During World War II Americans were constantly exhorted to sacrifice for the war effort. In reality most civilians saw dramatic improvements in their level of comfort and security between 1941 and 1945. The experience of fighting a total war turned the United States into the most powerful and prosperous nation in the world.

In 1941 President Roosevelt called on the United States to become the "great arsenal of democracy." But with the U.S. economy just coming out of a 10-year-long slump, many manufacturers were reluctant to retool their factories for defense production. For the first time since the start of the Great Depression they were making good money selling consumer goods to civilians. In 1941 American allies were desperate for planes, tanks, and other weapons, and American soldiers on field maneuvers drove trucks labeled "tank" instead of the real thing, while American factories turned out a million more civilian automobiles than they had in 1939. It took a level of government intervention in the economy never before seen in American history to get assembly lines in Detroit and other industrial centers producing the thousands of tanks and planes victory required.

In the months after Pearl Harbor Roosevelt set up many new government agencies to oversee the economy. The War Production Board, established in January 1942, was given the responsibility of converting American industry to war production. The board used both a stick and a carrot to get reluctant manufacturers to begin producing war materials. It issued orders forbidding the use of scarce resources in nonmilitary production, such as civilian automobiles. But it also offered industry tax breaks, loans, guaranteed profits, and other incentives. During the Second World War the federal government paid for much of the expansion of the nation's industrial capacity. As Secretary of War Henry L. Stimson commented, "If you are going to try to go to war, or to prepare for a war, in a capitalist country, you have got to let business make money out of the process or business won't work." Once they overcame their hesitation to give up producing for the civilian market, business leaders found that the war offered them the opportunity to make record-breaking profits.

Other government agencies were set up to deal with specific economic problems. The War Manpower Commission, organized in April 1942, was in charge of recruiting workers for defense industries. The National War Labor Board settled disputes between labor and management. The Office of Price Administration fixed maximum prices for consumer goods to hold down inflation. It was in charge of rationing— that is, limiting the amounts of gasoline, sugar, coffee, canned food, shoes, and other scarce goods that civilians could buy. Other government agencies were established to oversee the operation of the petroleum, shipping, transportation, and rubber industries.

The rubber industry provides an example of how government intervention in the economy worked. Rubber was a vital military commodity. The army could not move without rubber for the tires on its jeeps and trucks, nor could its soldiers march without rubber for the soles of their boots. Before the war the U.S. imported most of its rubber from the Dutch East Indies and Malaya, sources that were cut off by Japanese conquest at the start of the war. In the months after Pearl Harbor the

Children looking for the War Ration Book Two point values of canned and bottled foods *(Franklin D. Roosevelt Library)*

frightening prospect of the United States exhausting its rubber supplies was a very real one.

The government followed a dual strategy to ease the rubber crisis. New regulations forced the public to save on the chief form of civilian

Nose cones for bombers were manufactured by women workers at Douglas Aircraft's Long Beach, California, Plant. *(National Archives)*

rubber consumption, automobile tires. In 1942 the Office of Price Administration introduced gasoline rationing. Families were given stamps entitling them to buy a limited amount of gasoline every week. By 1943 the average American car was being driven a third less than in 1941. This saved rubber as well as gasoline, since the fewer miles a car spent on the road, the longer its tires would last. The government also spent hundreds of millions of dollars to build 51 brand-new factories to produce synthetic rubber. Synthetic rubber had been invented during World War I, but had proven too expensive to develop and market in the years between the wars. After building these new factories, the government then turned them over to U.S. rubber companies for a small fee. The government thus paid for the development costs that industry itself was reluctant to pay. By 1944 nearly 90 percent of all rubber used in the United States was being produced in these government-built factories.

The government's wartime intervention in the economy was not always a model of efficiency, but in the end it did the job. Thanks to the free-flowing federal spending on the war, American manufacturing output doubled from 1939 to 1944. Giant new factories sprang into existence, like the mile-long Ford airplane plant in Willow Run, Michigan, employing 42,000 workers at peak wartime employment. Miracles of production were achieved, like Henry Kaiser's shipyards that cut down construction time on cargo vessels from 355 days to 56 days per ship between 1941 and 1942. All told, the United States produced 100,000 tanks and armored cars, 300,000 airplanes, 41 billion rounds of ammunition—and two atomic bombs—by 1945. This amounted to more than 30 percent of the weapons and munitions used against the Germans and Italians, and almost 90 percent of those used against the Japanese.

None of this came cheaply. At the height of the war the government was spending $250 million a day on war expenses. Total federal spending increased from under $9 billion in 1939 to $95.2 billion by 1945. The Treasury Department faced unprecedented problems in coming up with the revenue to pay for all this. Much of it, in fact, would not be paid for during the war. The national debt increased from $43 billion to almost $260 billion by 1945. Some of the expense of the war was met by raising income taxes. To collect taxes more efficiently, the payroll withholding system was introduced. For the first time wage-earners paid off their tax bills throughout the year with the money withheld from their paychecks. The number of people paying taxes also increased dramatically. Before the war only very well-off people paid federal taxes; by the end of the war the system had expanded to tax virtually the entire workforce. The number of taxpayers increased from 7 million in 1940 to 42 million in 1945.

Few people were happy to pay taxes, but the Treasury Department thought up another way of raising money that was much more popular. That was through the sale of war bonds. By purchasing a bond, which would be paid off by the government after a fixed number of years, Americans were lending the Treasury Department the money to fight the war. Since bonds were seldom as profitable as other forms of investment, the government had to rely on patriotic appeals and public relations hoopla to make them attractive.

"You're exhausted thinking up reasons why *not* to buy War Bonds . . ." the text of one war bond advertisement in a magazine read, "while thousands of American boys are going without food and sleep to protect your hide." Above was a picture of a prosperous-looking civilian asleep on his living room couch. "If this doesn't apply to you, tear it out and send it to someone it does!" Where guilt failed to do the trick, glamor stepped in to lend a hand. Hollywood stars spoke at war bond rallies and on the radio to encourage Americans to buy bonds. Hollywood actress Betty Grable, the GI's favorite "pin-up girl" during the war, auctioned off her silk stockings to raise money for war bonds. Comedian Jack Benny auctioned off his violin. Through such techniques the Treasury Department was able to raise $10 billion in 1942, and billions more as the war continued. Although only a drop in the bucket in the war's total cost, the war bond drives had the added benefit of creating a sense of civilian participation in the war effort. The drives also helped hold down inflation by absorbing income that would have bid up the price of scarce consumer goods.

Most Americans wanted to do their bit to help the war effort. They bought war bonds. They planted 20 million vegetable "victory gardens" in their backyard to ease food shortages. They joined local civil defense committees and staged air raid drills. They gave blood to the Red Cross. They turned in their old pots and pans in government-sponsored aluminum scrap drives, and old raincoats and galoshes in rubber drives. But unlike British, Russian, Chinese, and other Allied civilians who faced bombing and much worse, Americans at home were sheltered from the real horrors of the war.

Americans suffered some inconveniences, like having no gasoline for the customary Sunday drive, or having to stand up on a crowded trainride. But apart from the servicemen (including the merchant marines) who actually risked their lives, the relatives of those killed and maimed in the war, and those Japanese Americans who were interned, World War I proved to be a time of vast improvement in the standard of living of most Americans. Thanks to government wartime spending, the Great Depression of the 1930s was laid to rest. Seventeen million new jobs were created during the war. Unemployment, which had never dropped below 12 percent during the 1930s, fell to 1.3 percent in 1943. Just about anyone who wanted a job could find one. Anyone who was dissatisfied with a job could quit and find another within a few days. Even with government regulations on wage increases, average yearly

Plowing Boston Common as part of the Victory Garden Program
(Franklin D. Roosevelt Library)

income—adjusted for inflation—jumped from $754 in 1940 to $1,289 in 1944. Farm income tripled during the war. People paid off old debts, bought houses, and put money in the bank or in savings bonds. They dreamed of what model car they would buy once the war was over and those factories in Detroit stopped producing fighter planes and returned to civilian production.

Nazi leaders told their people that they would have to choose between guns and butter. In Germany, as in much of the rest of the world, guns won out. In the United States, the Second World War brought guns *and* butter.

12

FREEDOM'S WAR AT HOME

In 1941 President Roosevelt had promised that World War II would be a war to promote the "Four Freedoms." But nations have rarely fought wars purely for idealistic reasons. Considering the enemies the United States faced in the Second World War, however, the American war effort came fairly close to living up to its billing. When American soldiers reached Europe in 1943 and 1944 they would be greeted as liberators. Closer to home, the war had a mixed impact on the freedoms of Americans. Some found that the war offered unprecedented opportunities for social advances. Others found themselves the victims of wartime intolerance. While some Americans died for freedom's cause overseas, others fought battles—not always successfully— to defend or extend the cause of freedom at home.

When men marched off to the war after Pearl Harbor, most women were left behind. What role were they to play in the war effort? Some argued that their role should be the same one that women had always played in time of war—to "keep the home fires burning" by caring for families. The percentage of women who worked outside the home had been slowly increasing in preceding decades. But prejudices against working women—and especially against married working women— were still powerful. These feelings were reinforced during the depression when many believed that every married woman who worked was taking a job that could go to an unemployed man. Some states even passed laws restricting the jobs married women could take. When women did work outside the home, they were usually confined to jobs

With all able-bodied men at war, women's work included mechanical repair of airplanes. *(Library of Congress)*

that fit traditional views of a woman's role as helper and caregiver—teacher, nurse, domestic servant, retail clerk, and so on.

With the drafting of millions of men, industry soon faced a labor shortage. Responding to the crisis, the War Manpower Commission and private employers launched campaigns to attract women to industrial work. Women were called on to "back the attack" by taking over the jobs men had left behind. Wartime propaganda stressed that there was nothing "unfeminine" about women taking heavy industrial jobs. Norman Rockwell drew a famous portrait of a female war worker for the cover of the *Saturday Evening Post,* celebrating "Rosie the Riveter." Rosie's bulging arm muscles were strong enough to handle a rivet gun, but she still took the time to properly put on her makeup.

Responding to patriotic appeals as well as the opportunity to make money, the number of women who worked outside the home leaped up during the war. Between 1941 and 1945 the proportion of working women increased from 27.6 percent to 37 percent of all women.

Women abandoned low-paying jobs like domestic service for relatively high-paying jobs in factories and shipyards as welders, riveters, and machine operators. In 1940 only 10 percent of women who worked were employed in factories; by 1944 that figure had jumped to 30 percent. The rise in married women's participation in the labor force was particularly notable. During the war, for the first time ever they outnumbered single women in the workforce.

It was not always easy for women to take advantage of wartime employment opportunities. Married women with families were hard-pressed to find adequate care for their young children. They also had to put in a "double day," looking after their families' needs at night after putting in eight or 10 hours at a factory during the day. On the job they often had to face hostility from male workers (who feared competition from women workers after the war) and pay discrimination from employers. Women workers and some unions fought for the principle of equal pay for equal work, but met with limited success. A survey of 25 important wartime industries showed that women workers were paid on average 50 percent of what male workers earned.

Despite such hardships, wartime polls revealed that a majority of women who had taken jobs during the war wanted to keep them once the war was over. But the old prejudices against women working had been shelved only temporarily. As the war came to a close, government and industry spokesmen argued that women should accept that they were working only "for the duration." Once the men came marching home, they should willingly return to the home (or to the lower-paid jobs they formerly held). After the war the number of women working outside the home dropped, but never as low as the prewar levels. For millions of "Rosie the Riveters," the war had proven that they could compete in a man's world. The long-range effects of the wartime experience could be seen in the 1970s when, for the first time ever, a majority of American women would work outside the home. By that time it no longer seemed strange or "unfeminine" that they should do so.

Talk about the "Four Freedoms" sounded ironic to many of the nation's 13 million black citizens when the United States went to war in 1941. Through most of the American South, where the overwhelming majority of blacks then lived, they were denied the right to vote or to sit on juries. Blacks were forced to send their children to separate and inferior public schools. They had to ride in the back of the bus or on separate "Jim Crow" cars on trains.

Nor was discrimination confined to the South. In northern cities, where blacks lived in rundown neighborhoods like New York's Harlem and Chicago's South Side, conditions were not much better. Blacks held the worst-paying jobs, could not rent apartments or buy houses in white neighborhoods, and were often refused service in restaurants and at lunch counters. Americans condemned the Nazi theories of racial superiority, but many whites still subscribed to their own set of racist beliefs. Blacks protested the Red Cross practice of segregating blood donated in blood drives into "white" and "colored" blood, a distinction that makes no scientific sense. The protesters were denounced by some in Congress as "crackpots" who were scheming "to mongrelize this nation."

To challenge such beliefs, A. Philip Randolph, president of the all-black Brotherhood of Sleeping Car Porters, organized the March on

A. Philip Randolph, labor leader who helped to found the Brotherhood of Sleeping Car Porters *(National Archives)*

Washington movement in the spring of 1941. The brotherhood's slogan was, "We loyal Negro American citizens demand the right to work and fight for our country." Randolph wanted the federal government to step in to end racial discrimination in employment in war industries and in the armed forces. If the government refused, he threatened to organize a march of 100,000 blacks in the streets of Washington.

The march was called off at the last moment when Roosevelt issued an executive order establishing the Fair Employment Practices Commission (FEPC) to fight discrimination in war industries. It was an important symbolic victory, because it was the first time since just after the Civil War that the federal government had promised to take action on behalf of the civil rights of black Americans. But the FEPC was never given adequate powers or enough funding to make much of an impact against employment discrimination. Nor had Roosevelt done anything about the military services, which remained segregated throughout the war.

War did bring new opportunities to blacks. The same conditions of labor scarcity that benefited women also helped blacks find jobs in factories and shipyards. Between 1942 and 1945 the percentage of blacks among war workers increased from 3 percent to 8 percent; 400,000 blacks left the South for jobs in the industrial centers of the north and west. But blacks met even greater hostility from white workers than did women workers. In the crowded industrial cities, blacks and whites competed for scarce housing and recreation facilities. Whites feared that after the war, when jobs were less plentiful, they would have to compete with blacks for them. These tensions led to the outbreak of a bloody race riot in Detroit in June 1943. It took the U.S. Army to finally end the riot after three days of fighting that left 25 blacks and nine whites dead.

Although the war inflamed racial hatreds, it also laid the foundations for later gains in racial equality. The thousands of blacks pouring into northern cities were able to vote for the first time in their lives. Harlem elected its first black congressman, Adam Clayton Powell, Jr., during the war. Some white elected officials found it politically useful to become more supportive of the civil rights cause. In northern cities like Chicago, black civil rights activists and their white supporters began experimenting with "sit-in" tactics to force the desegregation of restaurants. When Martin Luther King, Jr., and others began to use similar tactics in the South in the 1950s and 1960s, the modern civil rights era was launched. American blacks did not enjoy anything like the "Four

Freedoms" at the end of the war, but they had started down a road that would lead to those freedoms.

Very few Americans opposed the Second World War. Public protests against the war were rare. Most conscientious objectors—those who claim their moral or religious conscience prevents them from serving in the military—agreed to accept some form of alternative service, as medics or in civilian work camps. Because so little protest was heard, there was not much public sentiment for punishing protesters. Unlike the First World War, the government did not close down newspapers or imprison people for their antiwar views. America's civil liberties record during the war would have been a good one—with one terrible exception. That was the roundup and internment of 110,000 people of Japanese descent living in the United States, two-thirds of them native-born American citizens.

During World War I, German Americans had been viewed by their fellow citizens with suspicion and hostility. Afterward, many Americans were ashamed of the way the German Americans had been mistreated. When the United States went to war against the Axis powers, the Roosevelt administration went out of its way to stress its belief in the loyalty of both German Americans and Italian Americans.

Only Japanese Americans found themselves treated more harshly. Unlike Americans of German and Italian background, Japanese Americans' rights were more easily attacked because they represented only a tiny minority of the American population. They also came from a non-European racial background, and were easily turned into scapegoats for America's Pacific defeats. Two weeks after Pearl Harbor, *Time* magazine ran an article entitled "How to Tell Your Friends from the Japs." The article contrasted the appearance of "kindly" Chinese allies and "arrogant" Japanese enemies:

> Those who know them best often rely on facial expression to tell them apart: the Chinese expression is likely to be more placid, kindly, open; the Japanese more positive, dogmatic, arrogant . . . Japanese are hesitant, nervous in conversation, laugh loudly at the wrong time . . . Japanese walk stiffly erect . . . Chinese more relaxed . . . sometimes shuffle.

On the West Coast, where most of the nation's Japanese Americans lived, hysterical fears of invasion and sabotage were whipped up by the regional army commander, Lt. Gen. John L. DeWitt. DeWitt charged

A "relocation center" for Japanese-American citizens *(National Archives)*

that Japanese Americans were signaling with radios and lights to off-shore aircraft carriers and submarines, preparing the way for an assault on the American mainland. In fact, as government agencies like the Federal Bureau of Investigation and the Office of Naval Intelligence knew at the time (and throughout the war), there was no evidence that Japanese Americans committed any acts of treason, sabotage, or espionage during World War II. But DeWitt was not interested in the evidence. As he argued with astonishing illogic in the spring of 1942: "The very fact that no sabotage has taken place to date is a disturbing and confirming indication that such action will be taken." DeWitt saw no point in trying to sort out aliens from native-born or the loyal from the disloyal: "A Jap's a Jap," he declared.

DeWitt, unfortunately, was not just an isolated crackpot. If there was nothing Americans could do to Japan in the spring of 1942 to avenge Pearl Harbor, there was a lot they could do to hurt the Japanese Americans. Demands for the rounding-up of all Japanese Americans began to be heard from West Coast politicians and newspapers. There was also an outcry from self-interested groups like California's Grower-Shipper Vegetable Association, which wanted to do away with competition from the hardworking Japanese-American farmers.

President Roosevelt, to his discredit, caved in to this pressure. He issued orders authorizing military authorities to round up all people of Japanese descent on the West Coast, citizens and aliens alike. The heads of Japanese families were ordered to register with the authorities on March 31, 1942. They were then given between a few days and a few weeks to dispose of their property and businesses. Most were forced to sell their farms, homes, and personal property for a fraction of their real value. Bringing only what they could carry by hand, Japanese families were sent to temporary assembly points like the Santa Anita race track near Pasadena, California, where they slept in horse stalls. Beginning in May 1942 they were transferred to 10 hastily built "relocation centers," a polite name for concentration camps. These were located in the nation's interior, like the Manzanar camp in the California desert.

The American concentration camps were different from the Nazi concentration camps in Europe. Inmates were not killed, starved, beaten, or otherwise mistreated once they were behind barbed wire. But

Detainees at the Manzanar Relocation Center, Manzanar, California
(National Archives)

there was one uncomfortable similarity between the two. Japanese-American men, women, and children, like the Jews in Europe, were being collectively punished simply because they had been born into minority. Some were eventually released to work in other parts of the country, and others enlisted in the American military. Most would remain imprisoned until the end of the war, when they were given $25 and a train ticket home to rebuild their shattered lives.

War is a time of social change—and social strain. Wars give birth to idealism—and to intolerance. Freedom's cause suffered defeats as well as victories on the American home front in World War II.

13
OVER THERE, OVERSEAS

For millions of Americans, overseas service in World War II was the first opportunity they ever had to visit a foreign land. These were the days before inexpensive and frequent commercial airline flights to other parts of the world. Foreign travel was a luxury enjoyed mostly by the well-to-do. The war thrust Americans into new and often exotic settings. Some found it exciting; others found it unsettling. Homesickness was a widespread complaint. Voluntary organizations like the Red Cross and the USO (United Services Organization) did what they could to ease the stay of Americans abroad. Civilians in the host countries where GIs were stationed often extended warm welcomes. Going to war was certainly no holiday, but many GIs returned home with fond memories of at least some of their time overseas.

The crews of bombers and transport planes flew across the Atlantic to Europe, or hop-skipped their way by air to Hawaii, Australia, and other Pacific locations. But most U.S. fighting men traveled to overseas assignments aboard ship. Nearly 1 million soldiers and marines were shipped overseas in 1942, followed by 2 million in 1943, and nearly 3 million in 1944. The great majority were sent to Europe. In the early years of the war most men were shipped overseas in the units they had trained with. Units scheduled for overseas duty were transferred from training bases to ports of embarkation like Boston, New York, Hampton Roads (Virginia), and San Francisco. They boarded the troopships loaded down with packs, weapons, and duffel bags. The last memory many carried with them from the shores of America was the sound of a military band playing vintage World War I tunes like "Over There."

For some GIs, the worst part of the war was about to unfold. The trip to Europe in slow-moving convoys could take two weeks or even longer. (The few who made the trip abroad refitted luxury liners such as the *Queen of Elizabeth* or *Queen Mary* were much luckier, usually reaching England in five or six days.) The cramped quarters in the holds of the ships allowed no privacy and little comfort. Men slept in narrow bunk beds stacked as many as six deep. On especially crowded ships they had to sleep in shifts. Mealtime came twice a day and required waiting in long lines to be served food that had to be eaten standing up. GIs traveling on British ships found themselves confronted in the morning with unfamiliar breakfast items like kippered herring or kidney stew. These did not go down well with those already feeling queasy from seasickness. Some men lost 25 pounds on the trip overseas.

Everyone who shipped abroad was issued a life jacket and assigned to a lifeboat in the event of German submarine attack. In fact, there were seldom enough lifeboats. Relatively few men lost their lives in U-boat attacks while being shipped to Europe, but no one who stepped up the gangplank in New York or Hampton Roads could be entirely sure that he would see dry land again. As the long days passed, they spent their time reading, writing letters, or gambling. (A few lucky ones left the troop ships considerably wealthier than when they had boarded.) As a rule the troops were not told their destination until they arrived in their final port. If they shipped out from the West Coast it was pretty clear that they were not heading for Europe. If they shipped out from the East Coast they could usually figure out, by the kind of clothing they were issued, whether they were heading for Iceland, Africa, or England.

In some of the lands where Americans were stationed they had little or no chance for contact with the civilian population—assuming there even was a civilian population. Certainly that was true for the soldiers stationed in the wintry Aleutian islands off the coast of Alaska, and for those who found themselves on some of the more desolate locations in the Pacific. In China, India, and North Africa there were plenty of civilians around, but they belonged to cultures that seemed utterly strange and unsympathetic to the GIs. On the European continent, despite the language barrier, the GIs' contact with civilians was much friendlier. For the frontline soldiers, however, contact was necessarily brief. One French resident of the village of Lagny-sur-Marne described the arrival of American GIs hard on the heels of retreating Germans in August 1944:

> For four years Lagny had been awaiting this moment . . . People broke out bottles they'd carefully hoarded for the day of victory, and they offered drinks all around . . . Hugged and kissed and tugged at, the Americans took it all as best they could . . . We offered them tomatoes and wine, and they passed to us chewing gum and all sorts of little packages of chocolate and candy and Camel cigarettes—how good they were!

Because the war was still far from over and there were more Germans to fight and other villages down the road to be liberated, the Americans moved on from Lagny-sur-Marne before their welcome could wear out.

The GIs had their most sustained contact with civilians in countries where they shared the same language and culture, Australia and in the United Kingdom (including England, Scotland, and Northern Ireland). Tens of thousands of Americans were stationed in or passed through Australia on their way to other battlefronts. By early June 1944 there were more than 1.5 million U.S. servicemen in Great Britain. The first Americans got the heartiest welcomes. The British had expected a German invasion in 1940 and 1941. To see American troops arriving in 1942 meant that the days of standing alone on the defensive were over. Families competed with one another to invite a "Yank" to tea or dinner. When GIs visited the local pubs they rarely got the chance to spend their own money, so eager were the locals to buy them drinks.

The army took the precaution of issuing to each American sent to the United Kingdom the military equivalent of a tourist guidebook. The book was filled with helpful tips like, "The British don't know how to make a good cup of coffee. You don't know how to make a good cup of tea—It's an even swap." There was a lot the Americans had to learn about the "Limeys," as they called the English. They had to get used to the warm beer in the pubs, the constant rain, the strange new money system, the lack of central heating, and the British custom of driving on the "wrong" (left-hand) side of the road. Britons had to get used to American noise, energy, and ever-increasing visibility. Americans were curious about the countries they visited, but they were also eager for the sights and sounds of home. The British radio network, the BBC, tried to make the GIs feel more at home with regular broadcasts of sports news from the United States. The USO sponsored tours by Hollywood celebrities to entertain American troops at home and abroad. Comedians such as Bob Hope and Martha Raye, and singers such as the Andrews Sisters were especially popular. One of the Andrews Sisters' biggest wartime hits was a song called "Boogie Woogie Bugle Boy," which included the stanza:

> He was a famous trumpet man from out Chicago way,
> He had a boogie sound that no one else could play.
> He was top man at his craft.
> But then his number came up and he was called in the draft.
> He's in the army now a-blowin' reveille.
> He's the boogie woogie bugle boy of Company B.

The American Red Cross sent more than 2,000 volunteers to run hundreds of clubs in England. These clubs offered GIs snack bars, dances, games, and libraries. Red Cross coffee and doughnuts were a favorite treat for GIs in England.

The Americans brought chewing gum, chocolate bars, Coca-Cola, silk stockings, and other scarce or exotic items. These made the GIs popular with the children who flocked around them—and the women they dated. The Americans built a reputation among young women in the British Isles as smooth talkers and unfaithful companions. It was not entirely undeserved. Still, about 80,000 GIs would marry British "war brides" during the war; another 15,000 married Australians. But the GIs' popularity with local women—and the not entirely unrelated fact that they were paid about four times as much as the average British soldier—led to some bad feelings and an occasional brawl between allies. "Oversexed, overpaid, and over here," was a common saying about the Americans, as the early welcome began to cool. Similar feelings surfaced in Australia, with one poet complaining: "They saved us from the Japs/Perhaps/But at the moment the place is too Yankful/For us to be sufficiently thankful."

American women were few and far between overseas. Each branch of the military services organized a women's unit during the war, with 140,000 joining the Women's Army Corps (WACs). The women worked in clerical, communications, supply, and educational jobs, replacing men who could be released for combat duties. But none of the military services allowed women to go overseas until 1943. At peak strength,

OVER THERE, OVERSEAS

Bing Crosby, stage, screen, and radio star, sings to Allied troops at the opening of the London Stage Door Canteen in Piccadilly, London, England. *(National Archives)*

there were only 7,500 WACs in the entire European theater of operations, fewer still in the Pacific. There were also several thousand army nurses in Europe, some of whom served just behind the front lines, caring for wounded men while enemy shells and bombs fell around them.

One sensitive issue complicating American-British relations during the war was the presence of a sizable number of black American GIs stationed in England. Not that the English objected to the blacks. Quite the opposite. They could not understand why blacks were treated so poorly in the American military, and refused to honor the segregationist customs of white Americans.

The United States fought the Second World War with a racially segregated armed forces. At the start of the war blacks were not even accepted in the air corps or the marines, or in the navy except as stewards (servants) aboard ship. The army accepted black soldiers, but only for noncombat occupations such as construction, transportation, and supply. The military's racist attitude ignored the long and heroic history of black participation in America's wars. It also ignored the example of Dorie Miller, a steward aboard the USS *West Virginia*, who put down his mop and picked up a machine gun during the Japanese attack at Pearl Harbor. He downed an attacking Japanese plane, for which he was honored with the Navy Cross.

When blacks joined the army, they were not treated with the respect that was paid other men in uniform. In the South they continued to be kept out of restaurants and forced to ride in the back of the bus. Several bloody race riots, with both sides armed, broke out on American military bases in 1942 and 1943. It was only late in the war, with American casualties steadily mounting, that blacks found more acceptance. The navy, marines, and air corps all began to accept black recruits; there was even one all-black pilot unit in the air corps. The army began to organize black combat units, although it kept them under the command of white officers. Finally, during the Battle of the Bulge, the army sent

Black soldiers attend a class for radio operators. *(Library of Congress)*

Tuskegee Airmen

ON THE EVE OF WORLD WAR II, THE U.S. ARMY AIR Corps refused to accept any African-American recruits. Finally, under legal and political pressure from Washington, the air corps agreed to organize several segregated squadrons. The most famous of these was the Ninety-ninth Fighter Squadron, which trained at a segregated facility in Tuskegee, Alabama. The 1,000 black pilots trained there became known as the Tuskegee Airmen and were also referred to as the "Black Eagles." In April 1943 the Ninety-ninth Fighter Squadron was deployed to North Africa under the command of Lt. Col. Benjamin O. Davis, Jr., (a West Point graduate who would go on to become the first black major general in the U.S. Army). The Black Eagles became the first group of black pilots in combat and racked up a distinguished record in fighting the air war over Italy. All told, by war's end the Tuskegee pilots were credited with shooting down 111 German planes.

black volunteers to fight alongside whites in the same companies. But these blacks were still kept segregated in separate platoons.

When black soldiers got to Britain, they found themselves treated as equals by local civilians, who were white. They were welcomed into pubs and restaurants, and they did not have to ride on the back of the bus when they took public transportation. It was an eye-opening experience, particularly for blacks from the South, to learn that two races could live side by side as equals. The blacks could even date English women if they wanted to, though the sight of black men and white women together provoked some white GIs to violence. "I don't mind the Yanks," ran a familiar English joke during the war, "but I can't say I care for those white chaps they've brought with them."

In the First World War "Over There" meant the trenches of France, and most American soldiers spent only a few months there before the war had ended. In the Second World War "overseas" could mean anywhere from Casablanca to Chungking, in a war that lasted almost four years. By the time the war ended, Americans would be aware of the wide and different world that surrounded them as never before in their history.

14
THE SECRET WAR

When World War II broke out, the United States was the only one of the major powers that lacked a central intelligence service. The idea of spying in peacetime was distasteful to American leaders. In 1931 Secretary of State Henry Stimson (who later became secretary of war in the Roosevelt administration) refused to consider a proposal to establish an American espionage agency: "Gentlemen," he declared, "do not read each other's mail."

The army and the navy maintained their own intelligence units, but their efforts were haphazard and uncoordinated. There were some intelligence triumphs in the prewar era, most notably the breaking of the Japanese diplomatic code. But the United States had made no systematic effort to learn about the weapons, tactics, industrial capabilities, or culture of its potential enemies. After Pearl Harbor Americans had to rush to catch up with their enemies and their allies in the art of waging the "secret war" of espionage and sabotage.

Fortunately for Americans, their British allies did not share their reluctance to engage in spying. British intelligence had two branches: MI5, which was in charge of military espionage, and the Special Operations Executive (SOE), in charge of sabotage and other secret operations behind enemy lines. They were the equal or superior of the German military intelligence service, the *Abwehr*, and the notorious Nazi secret police, the Gestapo.

In 1939, just months before the start of the Second World War, British intelligence scored one of the greatest coups in the history of

THE SECRET WAR

Machine for
deciphering
Japanese "Purple"
diplomatic code
(National Archives)

espionage. The German military coded its radio messages by means of an electrically operated coding machine called Enigma. With the aid of the Polish secret service, the British acquired one of the Enigma machines and put together a team of their top mathematicians and cryptoanalysts to figure out how it worked. Because of their success, British and American military strategists were able to read the most top-secret German military plans as they were broadcast to German commanders in the field. The intelligence gathered through the use of the Enigma machine was code-named "Ultra."

Through Ultra, Britain had advance warning of the *Luftwaffe*'s plans for the Battle of Britain, Rommel's plans for his campaigns in North Africa, and the German airborne invasion of Crete. The British and Americans planned their invasions of Sicily and Normandy knowing the strength and location of most of the German units they would have to fight. Ultra helped the Royal Navy chase down the German warship *Bismarck* in the Atlantic, and gave British and American convoy commanders warnings of U-boat ambushes.

Ultra also helped the Allies pull off an elaborate hoax in 1943, when they were preparing the invasion of Sicily. They dressed a corpse in a British officer's uniform, attached a briefcase to its wrist with a chain, and floated it onto a Spanish beach. The briefcase contained documents indicating that the Allies' next blow in the Mediterranean would fall either on the island of Sardinia or in Greece. Spanish authorities passed the documents on to the Germans, who were convinced they were authentic. As a result, Hitler diverted troops from Sicily to Greece to guard against an invasion that never came. The Allies knew, through Ultra, that Hitler had fallen for the trick.

In itself, Ultra did not determine the outcome of the war. Even with advance warning of Rommel's intentions, for example, the British still had great difficulty in dealing with the "Desert Fox" in North Africa. But the eventual Allied victory could have proven far more costly without Ultra.

Americans made a similar breakthrough, contributing substantially to victory in the Pacific, through an espionage program code-named Magic. The Japanese, like the Germans, used an encoding machine. Their machine was called Purple. Army cryptoanalysts, under the direction of the brilliant intelligence officer Col. William Friedman, broke Japan's diplomatic code in 1940. They were able to reconstruct a Purple machine without ever having seen one. Navy cryptoanalysts also broke sections of the Japanese naval operational code, although a change in the code shortly before the start of the Pacific war threw American intelligence off the scent of Pearl Harbor. By the spring of 1942, however, American experts had cracked the new code, in time to be of use in the battle of the Coral Sea. Magic made possible the great American victory at Midway, because virtually every aspect of the enemy's plan of attack was known to U.S. naval commanders in advance. American signal experts also made use of a system known as traffic analysis, keeping track of enemy warships by means of the location, volume and pattern of messages they sent.

Magic had not been able to prevent the surprise attack on December 7, but it did help Americans avenge themselves on the architect of the Pearl Harbor attack, Admiral Yamamoto. On April 17, 1943, U.S. Naval Intelligence learned through decoded radio messages that Yamamoto was leaving the Japanese base at Rabaul by plane for an inspection tour of Japanese bases on other islands. Yamamoto was known for his extreme punctuality, which proved to be his downfall. His plane was scheduled to land at 9:45 the next morning at Kahili, a Japanese base on the south end of the island of Bougainville. A squadron of U.S. Army P-38 fighters flew from Guadalcanal on April 18 to intercept the bomber carrying Yamamoto, a second bomber carrying his staff, and the half-dozen Zero fighters that guarded them.

With split-second timing the Americans intercepted Yamamoto's party, attacked from above and below, and shot down the two bombers. Yamamoto died as his plane crashed in flames on the island below. The Japanese chalked up the attack to bad luck, failing to realize that their codes were being read.

In June 1942 President Roosevelt signed an executive order creating a new government agency, the Office of Strategic Services. The OSS was given a complicated assignment. It would conduct espionage, research, and analysis of the enemy's military and industrial capabilities. It would also undertake assignments behind the enemy lines to aid resistance movements and damage the fighting capabilities and morale of Axis forces. Roosevelt appointed William J. "Wild Bill" Donovan as OSS director. Donovan, a New York corporate lawyer who had won the Medal of Honor for Heroism in the First World War, assembled a force that ultimately grew to some 13,000 agents. OSS was a unique mixture of civilians and soldiers, including European refugees, college professors, American veterans of the Spanish Civil War, Wall Street lawyers, Hollywood stuntmen, and even some gangsters. All kinds of skills were going to be needed in the OSS's secret war.

One of the most important and complicated jobs of the OSS was to establish contact with and provide aid to resistance movements within Axis-occupied countries. German and Japanese military triumphs in the years between 1939 and 1942 had brought much of the European and Asian continents under Axis control. But the conquerors had not won the hearts and minds of the conquered peoples. Resistance movements, also known as the underground, sprang up throughout Europe and Southeast Asia. These movements provided invaluable aid to the Allied cause by spying on the enemy, sabotaging transportation, industrial, and military facilities, and aiding the escape of downed Allied airmen and prisoners of war. Some resistance groups took to the hills, forests, and jungles to launch full-scale guerrilla wars against the occupiers; others stayed in populated areas to rally civilian resistance. Many German and Japanese troops, who would otherwise have been free to fight Allied armies, were tied down during the war, guarding railroads and factories or chasing guerrillas.

Aiding resistance movements could be a tricky business, because these movements were interested in more than defeating the Axis occupiers. Many were also intent on shaping the postwar governments in their countries. All kinds of people with differing political ideas joined the resistance. Sometimes they fought among themselves as well as against the Axis powers. Guns and ammunition provided to kill Germans and Japanese could just as easily be used to launch a revolution once the war was over. In Europe and Asia some of the most effective resistance movements were led by communists. Although the United States was allied with the Soviet Union against a common enemy, that did not guarantee it looked favorably on armed communist movements springing up in Axis-occupied countries. Time and again in dealing with resistance movements around the world, OSS agents were faced with difficult choices in deciding whom to aid and how to aid them.

In North Africa, for example, the Allies had made an alliance of convenience with the Vichy sympathizer Admiral Darlan. Just because Darlan had officially switched sides did not make him a democratic leader. His government kept many genuine antifascists in prison after the Allied landings. OSS agents in North Africa conspired to free prisoners from Darlan's concentration camps in order to recruit them for secret operations in Europe.

In Yugoslavia, the OSS provided support by air and sea to two rival guerrilla armies, the royalist Chetniks and the Communist partisans. The partisans were led by a man named Josip Broz, or "Tito," who after the war became the leader of Communist Yugoslavia. Different OSS officers on the scene developed rival loyalties to the two groups. Hollywood actor Sterling Hayden, an OSS lieutenant during the war, set up a fleet of boats to run supplies from southern Italy through the German blockade to an island, off the coast of Yugoslavia, held by partisans. He later recalled the "tremendously close personal feeling" he had developed for the partisans, who had "fought in spite of reprisals, had fought through bitter winters high in the mountains, with little clothing, next to no food, and only the arms they could scrape from the backs of their foes." Other OSS agents, including Allen Dulles, who would later head up the postwar-created Central Intelligence Agency (CIA), felt it was a mistake to give any aid to the partisans. In Italy, communists, socialists, monarchists, and even elements of Mussolini's old secret police vied for support from the OSS. There were similar differences among Americans as to who most deserved their support.

The European resistance movement that got the most attention from the Allies was the French underground. When the Allies in 1943 laid definite plans for the invasion of France, the British SOE and the American OSS stepped up their efforts to aid the French resistance. In a program code-named "Sussex," OSS and SOE sent 50 two-person teams of French agents into northern France to gather military intelligence in preparation for the invasion. After the invasion began in 1944, OSS and SOE launched a new program called Jedburgh. Specially trained three-person teams, consisting of one OSS or SOE officer, one French officer, and a British or American radio officer, were dropped by parachute behind German lines in France to contact, arm, and train French resistance fighters. The Jedburgh teams were able to do considerable damage to the Germans, at the risk of almost-certain torture and execution if they were captured by the Gestapo.

In the war against Japan, General MacArthur kept the OSS out of the southwestern Pacific theater. MacArthur set up his own intelligence system, which used radio-equipped coast watchers in the Solomon Islands to keep track of Japanese naval operations. His unit also provided supplies by air and submarine to some of the 200,000 Filipino

Jedburgh teams in front of B-24 just before takeoff in the obscurity of night. Area T, Harrington Airdrome, England, 1944. *(National Archives)*

guerrillas who fought the Japanese in the Philippines. But MacArthur did not want any competition from Donovan's men.

The OSS did play a significant role on the Asian mainland. In Burma the OSS organized its own guerrilla army, Detachment 101, which recruited 10,000 Kachin natives from the Burmese hills to wreak havoc behind Japanese lines. Before the war ended they had inflicted 5,500 casualties on the enemy, while rescuing 200 Allied airmen. OSS agents in Thailand set up an intelligence network that reached into Japan by means of the Thai embassy in Tokyo, reporting on the effectiveness of American air raids.

In Vietnam OSS officers came to the aid of a guerrilla force called the Viet Minh, which was fighting the Japanese while also preparing to fight for Vietnamese independence from France after the war. The Americans brought small arms and helped train the Viet Minh fighters, who in return provided intelligence and rescued downed American fliers. An OSS medic helped save the life of the Viet Minh's leader, Ho Chi Minh, who was suffering from malaria when the Americans met him in his jungle camp. The close wartime relations between the Americans and Ho Chi Minh were not destined to last. As the leader of Communist North Vietnam, Ho would challenge U.S. attempts to prop up a friendly government in South Vietnam in the 1960s. This led to the Vietnam War.

The United States fought World War II against one set of enemies, the Axis powers. But well before the final victory over Germany and Japan, new conflicts were taking shape. As the victorious allies approached Berlin, OSS agents in Europe had already begun to collect information that might prove useful in the event of a future war with the Soviet Union. The OSS itself did not survive the war, being disbanded by order of President Harry Truman in September 1945. As relations with the Soviet Union deteriorated fairly quickly, American leaders reconsidered their hasty action. In 1947 Congress authorized the creation of a new organization, the Central Intelligence Agency, which took up America's "secret wars" where the OSS had left off.

15

WAR IN ITALY

Salerno to the Rapido

There was something about the Italian campaign in the Second World War that veterans of the First World War found all too familiar. It was an infantryman's fight. The long, narrow Italian peninsula had few north-south roads, and the rugged Apennine Mountains ran through its center. It offered little opportunity for the kind of sweeping tank attacks that had characterized the fighting in North Africa. Allied infantry packed their supplies in by mule where trucks could not go, and on their backs where mules could not go. They had to launch a seemingly endless series of assaults on entrenched German positions. Like the trench assaults of the First World War's western front, the fighting in Italy—which was supposed to have been the "soft underbelly" of the Axis powers—proved a brutal war of attrition, a slow wearing down of the enemy.

In the summer of 1943 everything seemed to be going well for the Allies. The success of the Sicilian campaign had led to the overthrow of Italy's fascist dictator Mussolini. This made General Eisenhower and other American military strategists more willing to listen to British arguments to push on to the Italian mainland. Sensing defeat, the new Italian government headed by Field Marshal Badoglio was prepared to betray its German allies. Badoglio's agents made secret contacts with the Allies. On September 3 the Italians signed a secret surrender agreement to take effect when the Allies landed in force on the mainland.

Allied strategists initially considered the possibility of striking directly at Rome, through a combination of air and sea landings.

General Maxwell Taylor of the Eighty-second Airborne paid a secret visit to the Italian capital—already swarming with German troops—to investigate the possibility for a paratroop assault on the city's airports. In the end he recommended against the plan, but Allied strategists still looked forward to a rapid collapse of the country's resistance. As far as the Italians were concerned, the Allies were right to be optimistic. As soon as Italy's surrender was announced on September 8, Italian soldiers began to desert their positions. The Italian navy set sail from ports in Italy to surrender in North Africa and Malta. American troops aboard landing craft headed for Italian beaches cheered the news of the surrender, thinking it meant an easy landing ahead.

The Germans had other ideas. Hitler had stationed 16 divisions in Italy after the Sicilian invasion, and these would soon be reinforced by troops withdrawn from Corsica and Sardinia. German forces in northern Italy were commanded by Rommel, while those in the south were commanded by the less well known but very able Field Marshal Albert Kesselring. Initially the Germans believed that their best strategy would be a rapid withdrawal of all their troops to the "Gothic line" in northern Italy. (It ran roughly between Pisa and Rimini.) The battle of Salerno changed their plans.

Instead of the attack on Rome, Allied strategists decided on a two-pronged invasion of southern Italy. This attack would bring the Allies back in force to the European mainland for the first time since the British evacuation of France in 1940. Montgomery's Eighth Army would cross the Strait of Messina from Sicily in early September, in an operation code-named Baytown. That attack would be followed by Operation Avalanche. This would put Allied troops ashore along a wide beachhead in the Bay of Salerno, south of the major port city of Naples. The Salerno landings were entrusted to the U.S. Fifth Army (which included both American and British troops), under the command of Lt. Gen. Mark Clark. Clark, a veteran of the fighting in France in World War I, had served as Eisenhower's deputy in North Africa before receiving command of the Fifth Army.

Following a heavy artillery barrage, Montgomery's troops went ashore at the toe of Italy on September 3. They met no resistance. The troops landing at Salerno on September 9 were not as fortunate. The German Sixteenth Panzer Division was waiting for them in well-entrenched positions in the hills overlooking the invasion site. Americans, who were assigned to take the southern end of the bay, hit the beaches at 3:30 A.M. under heavy fire. Rockets fired from U.S. ships in the bay helped suppress enemy fire, but the U.S. advance depended as much on individual acts of bravery. Sgt. James M. Logan of the U.S. Thirty-sixth Division received the Medal of Honor for killing a squad of attacking Germans, then charging a German machine gun, killing its crew and turning the gun around to fire on the enemy.

The Germans hurled a tank assault at the Americans strung out along the exposed beaches at 7 A.M. With few U.S. tanks yet ashore, it was up to infantrymen with bazookas and grenades to stop them. By the end of the day Americans had fought their way four miles inland. British troops to their north had seized the town of Salerno. But a dangerous gap between the two armies along the beachfront had not been closed.

The Germans rushed reinforcements to the area, and plastered the beaches with attacks from fighters and bombers. The next week was a confusing chronicle of attacks and counterattacks, as the Allies and Germans traded control of strategic hills with heavy losses on both sides. At one point the Germans advanced to within two miles of the beach. General Clark began to consider pulling out American soldiers by boat. The Americans, however, reinforced by parachutists of the Eighty-second Airborne Division, were able to halt the Germans. Some of the hardest fighting took place on the hills west of Salerno where specially trained U.S. Rangers had landed on September 9. Outnumbered by counterattacking Germans, they fought a costly but successful three-week battle to hold the crucial hills surrounding the pass through which the Allies would need to go to reach Naples.

The two Allied armies now in Italy were slow to link up. British and American rivalries proved no less bitter in Italy than they had been in North Africa and Sicily. The cautious pace of Montgomery's advance from the south, slowed even more than usual by German bridge-blowing, infuriated Clark. The battle for Salerno was finally decided in the Allies' favor on September 18, when the Germans fell back to defensive lines farther north. The difficulty the Allies had in breaking out of the Salerno beachhead against a relatively weak defending force encouraged the Germans in a new strategy. They would resist the Allied advance all the way up the Italian peninsula. The Americans and British had gained a foothold in Italy, and also a foretaste of the kind of hard fighting that lay ahead. The Americans lost 500 dead, 1,800 wounded, and 1,200 missing in the nine-day battle for the Bay of Salerno, while the British suffered even heavier casualties.

An American-made Sherman tank, manned by a British crew, fords the Volturno River. Retreating Germans had blown up bridges to slow the Allied advance. *(National Archives)*

After finally linking up with Clark's forces, Montgomery's Eighth Army turned eastward to seize the airfield at Foggia on the eastern side of the peninsula. The Fifth Army pressed on to Naples, entering the city on October 1. German engineers wrecked the port by scuttling ships in the harbor, destroying docks and cranes, and mining a large part of the city. (A time bomb left in an Italian army barracks went off 10 days after the Allies entered Naples, killing 18 American paratroopers.) But within four days after entering the city, Allied engineers had cleared enough obstacles to allow the first U.S. supply ships to unload. Thereafter Naples became a major entry point for Allied troops and supplies.

With Italy's official surrender, and with the seizure of Naples and the airfield at Foggia (from which bombers could reach southern Germany), the Allies had won a great victory. They could have stopped where they were and turned all resources to preparing for next spring's invasion of France. But the momentum of the campaign fed a desire among Allied generals to drive on to capture still another glittering prize, Rome. It proved a costly decision.

The Germans were now digging in all up and down the Italian peninsula. They had gained a symbolic victory by snatching back Italy's former dictator Benito Mussolini in a daring glider raid on the mountain-top prison where he had been held since his arrest in late July. Mussolini no longer commanded any armies or the allegiance of his own country, but Hitler set him up in a puppet regime in the north of Italy. Rommel, who still wanted to see all German troops withdrawn from southern Italy, was sent off to France to prepare against the expected Allied invasion. Kesselring was given command of all German troops in the Italian theater.

As they pressed northward from Naples, the first major obstacle the Fifth Army ran into was the Volturno River, 250 to 300 yards wide and swollen by heavy rains. The Germans were dug in on the north bank. American and British troops reached the river on October 7 and launched their assault on October 12. Working under heavy fire, army engineers constructed specially made, metal Bailey bridges, which were designed to be bolted together quickly, like an Erector set. Troops were also ferried across on rafts and small boats or waded through the treacherous currents. It took three days to capture the north bank of the river. All that meant to the weary troops of the Fifth Army was that they had to press on until they faced the next river or mountain barrier.

Every time the Allies attacked, Kesselring held them up as long as possible, then pulled his troops back in a deliberate retreat to new defensive lines. By mid-January 1944 the two enemies confronted each other along the most daunting obstacle yet. This was known as the Gustav line, overlooking the Rapido and Garigliano Rivers, about halfway between Naples and Rome. The Germans had many months to get ready, digging their artillery into the rocky side of the mountains, shielding their machine-gun positions with armor plate, and strewing mines everywhere before their lines. The German defenses were centered on the town of Cassino, and behind it the craggy mountain called Monte Cassino. Kesselring predicted that the Allies "would break their teeth on it," and that proved no idle boast. The Allied assault virtually ground to a halt before the Gustav line.

The Allies sometimes referred to themselves as the "United Nations." Nowhere was that more evident than in the mixture of troops they had assembled for the Italian campaign. Americans fought alongside Britons, Canadians, Indian Gurkhas, New Zealanders, Poles, South Africans, Free French forces (including Algerians and Moroccans), Brazilians, and Italians. One of the American units that saw the hardest fighting was the U.S. 100th Battalion, made up entirely of Japanese Americans from Hawaii. Their motto was "Go for Broke," and they had crossed the Volturno River yelling "Banzai" to the amazement of the German defenders on the other side of the river. The 100th Battalion fought its way that fall and winter towards the Gustav line, suffering heavy casualties. It was joined in Italy in the spring of 1944 by the 442nd Regimental Combat Team, formed from Japanese-American volunteers from the West Coast war relocation camps. Together the 100/442nd became the most highly decorated unit in American military history.

One of the most popular men with the front line soldiers in Italy was the cartoonist for the U.S. Army newspaper *Stars and Stripes,* Bill Mauldin. He drew his cartoons at the front, often under fire, and tried to tell the story of the common foot soldier without sentimentalizing. In a collection of his cartoons published in 1944, he complained of people who returned from "quick tours" of the front. Such visitors often report that "the American soldier is the same clean-cut young man who left his home; others say morale is sky-high at the front because everybody's face is shining for the great Cause." That was not how Mauldin saw it. The soldiers that he shared foxholes with "are rough and their language gets coarse because they live a life stripped of convention and niceties . . . They wish to hell they were someplace else . . . But they stay in their wet holes and fight, and then they climb out and crawl through minefields and fight some more."

To break the Gustav line, the Americans would have to cross the fast-moving Rapido River. The Germans, dug in on the northern bank, had both sides of the river zeroed in with their guns. The assignment to cross the river was given to the U.S. Thirty-sixth Division, which had been in heavy combat since Salerno. The commander of the Thirty-sixth, Maj. Gen. Fred Walker, wrote in his diary after he received his orders, "We might succeed, but I do not see how we can."

The American attack began on the evening of January 20, 1944. Six thousand soldiers pulled rubber rafts and wooden boats from positions a mile from the river. They were under artillery fire the entire way. Only about 1,000 men made it across the river by boat. Army engineers had gotten a bridge up by 4 A.M., but it was knocked out by German shelling before more than a few hundred additional men got across. A second attack, even less successful than the first, was launched on the afternoon of January 21. Despite the smokescreen laid down by American artillery, German shells and machine guns were still able to rip into the boats on the river. The Americans on the far bank were cut off from supplies and reinforcements. The wounded died in their foxholes or drowned trying to get back to safety.

By the evening of January 22, all the remaining Americans on the Germans' side of the river had been killed or captured. The Germans had not even needed to call in their reserves to turn back the attack. Like a nightmare left over from World War I, more than 1,600 men were lost in an assault that had failed to gain an additional yard of enemy territory. It took another attack by the U.S. Thirty-fourth Infantry Division, at a cost of 2,200 men, to gain a permanent foothold on the north side of the Rapido. Once there, the Americans faced an even more formidable obstacle, Monte Cassino.

16

BREAKOUT
IN ITALY

The first four and a half months of fighting in Italy had been a frustrating time for the Allies. Although they gained control of southern Italy without great difficulty, their offensive had stalled well to the south of Rome. The Germans stubbornly held on along the Gustav line which bisected the middle of the Italian boot. They were proving themselves as skilled in defense as earlier in the war they had proved to be on the attack. In January 1944 the Allies launched a new assault, designed as an end run around the Gustav line. But Operation Shingle soon came to grief on the rocky beaches of Anzio. The disaster at Anzio was all too typical of the entire Allied campaign in Italy. The eventual triumph of the Allied armies in Italy was the product of superior resources, as well as the courage and fortitude of American and other troops who fought there. The victory was not due to the military brilliance of Allied commanders.

The idea of making an amphibious landing close to Rome had been discussed on and off by Allied strategists since the summer of 1943. Because of the difficulty of providing adequate air support until bases had been secured in southern Italy, the idea had been put aside in favor of concentrating on the landing at Salerno. Planning for the operation was revived in the late fall as the Allies approached the Gustav line, then dropped again as their offensive ground to a halt. But British prime minister Churchill was embarrassed by the lack of progress of the Allied armies in Italy—which had been his pet project all along. He insisted

U.S. tanks and a troop carrier move toward frontline positions near the Anzio beachhead, south of Rome. *(National Archives)*

that Operation Shingle be revived once again. The invasion, Churchill argued, would open a new road to Rome while forcing the Germans to withdraw troops from the Gustav line. Many remained doubtful about the operation's prospects for success, including Gen. John P. Lucas, commander of the U.S. VI Corps, whose troops were assigned to carry out the landings.

On January 22, 1944, 50,000 American and British troops landed on the beaches of Anzio and Nettuno, coastal towns about 30 miles south of Rome. At first all went well. The invasion came as a complete surprise to the Germans. Troops from the U.S. Third Division advanced between two and three miles inland on the first day. But their progress in the next few days was slow—due less to German opposition than to General Lucas's decision to consolidate the beachhead before heading inland. Lucas, like his British counterpart Montgomery, was a commander who believed in painstaking preparations for attack. He lacked the tanks that he felt were necessary for a rapid advance. By the third day since the invasion, the Allies had pushed only 10 miles inland. By the fourth day it was too late.

German field marshal Kesselring rushed eight divisions into the Alban Hills which lay between Anzio and Rome. Rather than stripping the Gustav line of soldiers, the Germans shifted troops from Yugoslavia, Germany, France, and northern Italy to plug the gap in their defenses. The heavy artillery they moved into the Alban Hills soon had the entire Anzio beachfront zeroed in. When Lucas finally launched his offensive, it smashed into a wall of German steel. The spearhead of Lucas's attack was a unit of 767 U.S. Rangers who marched under cover of darkness toward the city of Cisterna on January 30. At dawn they were ambushed by the Germans and virtually wiped out. Only six made it back to the beachhead.

The German counterattack came on February 16. Hitler hoped his soldiers could drive the Allies into the sea at Anzio. Then the Allies would be so discouraged that they would abandon plans for the invasion of France in 1944. The Germans knifed into the Allied lines, but were halted by a furious artillery barrage. Lucas's troops were able to hold off a second counterattack. But the bravery of the American and British troops at Anzio was not enough to save General Lucas's career. He was removed from command on February 22, and replaced by Gen. Lucian Truscott. Military historians have yet to agree on whether Lucas was merely the scapegoat for a fatally flawed plan decided on by his superiors or whether he threw away a chance to capture Rome months before the Allies finally reached the Eternal City.

In any case, the change of command had little practical effect. Allied troops at Anzio were under constant artillery and air attack. Soldiers put up signs by their sandbagged foxholes with sayings like "Beachhead Hotel: Special Rates to New Arrivals." There was no rear echelon in this battle; everyone was exposed to the dangers of the combat soldier's life. That included the doctors and nurses who continued to operate on wounded soldiers through the heaviest bombardments and whose hospital tents were repeatedly hit by German shells. Six of the almost 200 nurses who served at Anzio were killed. For nearly five months Allied troops endured the worst the Germans could throw at them. They were trapped in what "Axis Sally" (the Nazi propagandist who broadcast special radio programs designed to undermine the morale of Allied soldiers) called "the largest self-supporting prisoner-of-war camp in the world."

Now it was up to the Allied soldiers battling it out along the Gustav line to break through and save their brothers at Anzio. The key to cracking the Gustav line was to capture the town of Cassino and the high, rocky mountain that towered above it, Monte Cassino. Monte Cassino was a natural fortress, as St. Benedict, founder of the Benedictine monastic order, had known when he built his monastery there in A.D. 529. The monastery, destroyed and rebuilt several times in the centuries since then, was one of the historical treasures of the Roman Catholic Church. To the soldiers fighting and dying below, it looked like a German fort. In fact, the Germans had stayed out of the monastery. Their artillery spotters already had a fine view of the valley below. From their position they could call in directions to the German 88s and mortars located on surrounding hills.

On January 24, two days after the landings at Anzio, the U.S. Thirty-fourth Division fought its way across the Rapido River in the valley below Cassino. German guns hammered the Americans as they inched their way up rocky slopes toward Cassino. One American veteran of the fight, Lt. Harold Bond, later described the impact of the prolonged shelling:

> The air was filled with sound as if every German gun in the valley had fired toward us at the same time. We pushed down as far as we could in terror, and the ground all around us shook with gigantic explosions. Huge showers of earth rained down . . . The air was full of flying dirt and shrapnel. There was the frightening smell of gunpowder and crash after crash. I did not have time to wonder what was happening to my men. In such a shelling as this each man is isolated from everyone else. Death is immediately in front of him. He only knows that his legs and arms are still there and that he has not been hit yet; in the next instant he might be.

For almost three weeks the Americans fought on, but on February 12 the battered remnants of the Thirty-fourth were withdrawn and replaced by soldiers from Indian and New Zealand units.

The monastery at Monte Cassino fell victim to the Allies' frustration. Having no luck dislodging the Germans, they could at least destroy the building that had come to symbolize their helplessness. Despite the opposition of General Clark, the Allied Supreme Command decided to level the monastery. On February 15 more than 200 heavy and medium U.S. bombers dropped 576 tons of bombs on the monastery, reducing it to rubble. Three hundred Benedictine monks and refugees, who had ignored Allied leaflets warning of the attack, were killed. The Germans promptly moved into the rubble and set up machine guns and mortars, making Monte Cassino an even more powerful fortification than it had been before the attack. The destruction of the monastery also provided the Germans with a major propaganda victory. They were the ones usually accused of the needless destruction of civilian property and historical buildings.

After the bombing, the Indians and New Zealanders were no more successful than the Americans had been in their advance on Cassino. A third attack in March also failed. Success came only when the Allies deceived the Germans into thinking their next move would be another amphibious landing near Rome. This led Field Marshal Kesselring to withdraw some troops from the Gustav line. The Allied breakout came on May 11, spearheaded by French North African troops, who were supported by tanks from the U.S. First Armored Division. On May 18 Polish troops occupied the ruins of the monastery.

Cartoon by Bill Mauldin showing Willie, a World War II soldier, pointing a gun in the face of an enemy soldier, referring to the significant battle of Monte Cassino. *(Library of Congress)*

"Didn't we meet at Cassino?"

With the Germans falling back toward Rome, the Allied troops at Anzio made their own breakout on May 23. General Clark was ordered to use American forces from Anzio to block a crucial highway and encircle the retreating Germans. But Clark, who craved the glory of becoming known as the conqueror of Rome, disobeyed his orders. Ignoring the fleeing Germans, he sent his troops heading directly for Rome. Rome had been declared an open city by Field Marshal Kesselring. This meant that the Germans would not fight in its streets and thus spared it from destruction. The U.S. Army, with General Clark riding in a jeep at its head, rolled easily into Rome on June 4, ahead of its British rivals. Clark, unlike Hannibal in ancient times, had conquered Rome. Meanwhile the Germans escaped to fight another day.

The Allies continued to disagree over Italian strategy. Churchill, as always, wanted to press on with all available forces into northern Italy, and from there across the Alps into Austria or Yugoslavia. Roosevelt, as always, wanted to put more emphasis on the invasion of France. This time Roosevelt had his way. This was fortunate, because crossing the Alps could have proved even more difficult than cracking the Gustav line. Seven Allied divisions were withdrawn from Italy and sent to France.

Thanks in part to Allied air superiority, the troops that remained in Italy were able to continue their advance in the summer and early autumn of 1944. The Allies reached Florence on August 4, having advanced 270 miles in just over two months. German resistance was mild compared to the days when they held out along the Gustav line. But they continued to demolish bridges and ports, sowing deadly mines everywhere. In the port of Leghorn alone, Allied engineers had to disarm over 25,000 mines. In Florence the Germans dynamited all of the historic bridges that crossed the Arno River running through the center of the city, except for the magnificent Ponte Vecchio. Although sparing that architectural treasure, they blocked it at both ends by demolishing houses on either side of the river so that the debris fell onto the bridge.

After a brief halt in August to consolidate their gains, the Allies resumed a full-scale attack on September 10. Now the Allies were able to advance without great difficulty. The Germans no longer had the resources or the morale to put up the kind of fight they had made before the spring breakouts from Cassino and Anzio. They also faced a general uprising in their rear from the partisans, the name given to the

Jeep
VEHICLE AND ICON

THE JEEP WAS THE MOTORIZED WORKHORSE OF THE U.S. Army, a 54-horsepower, four-cylinder, quarter-ton 4 × 4 utility vehicle capable of carrying five passengers or a cargo of 800 pounds. Fully loaded, it got 20 miles to the gallon, and on good roads it could reach a speed of 60 miles an hour. Even more important, with four-wheel drive and a high clearance, it could travel off-road over rough terrain. It could be mounted with a .50 caliber machine gun or could tow a 37 mm antitank gun into action. Fitted with stretcher holders, it also served as a frontline ambulance. The name "jeep" came from the military designation for the vehicle, "general purpose," or "GP." The jeep was designed and built by the Willys-Overland Motors company in Toledo, Ohio, and was first adopted for military use in 1940. By the time the war was over, the jeep was one of the most widely and instantly recognized symbols around the world of America's military and industrial might. A famous Bill Mauldin cartoon from the war shows a U.S. Army sergeant, covering his face in grief, preparing to shoot his beloved jeep in the motor to put it out of its misery when it wound up crippled in an off-road accident.

Italians who fought the German army. Italian partisans cost the Germans as many as 5,000 casualties a month that summer. The Germans responded by killing 10 civilian hostages for every soldier they lost to partisan attacks. In one infamous massacre, 335 civilians were shot to death in a cave near Rome, in retribution for a partisan attack that killed 32 Germans. After the war Field Marshal Kesselring was sentenced to life imprisonment for the massacre.

The Allies' goal was to push the Germans out of the hills north of Florence and move down into the wide, flat Po Valley. There they would be able to deploy their tanks in mobile warfare and perhaps gain control over all of northern Italy up to the Alps. It was a race of troops and tanks against the annual winter rains. The rains came first, bogging down the Allied advance in the mud 10 miles short of the Po Valley. The campaign in Italy was effectively over for the year.

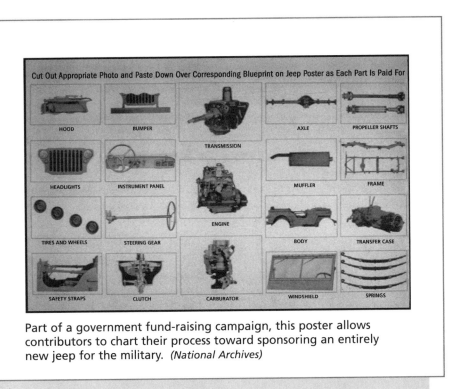

Part of a government fund-raising campaign, this poster allows contributors to chart their process toward sponsoring an entirely new jeep for the military. *(National Archives)*

The long road to Rome had cost the lives of 40,000 Allied soldiers; the Germans had lost half that number. Thousands more would die in the months of fighting that followed. From beginning to end, the Italian campaign had suffered from the mistakes and illusions of Allied leaders. Anzio and Cassino were strategic disasters. The capture of Rome on June 4 was a morale booster for the Allies, but it was overshadowed by the Normandy invasion which came two days later. By the summer of 1944, Italy became a theater of secondary importance to both the Allies and the Germans. The main action had shifted to France.

17

AIR WAR OVER EUROPE

Aerial combat was not entirely new. In the First World War airmen in rickety biplanes had engaged in spectacular "dog-fights" high over the trenches of the western front. Civilians had little to fear from such enemy air power, except for a few raids by German air-craft over English cities at the very end of the war. But in the Second World War, long before the first American soldiers were fighting and dying on the European mainland, Americans were carrying the war directly to Germany through the U.S. Army Air Force's strategic bomb-ing campaign. Early in the war both sides had decided that the system-atic bombing and destruction of their opponents' cities was a legitimate and necessary strategy for victory. There would be little distinction made between battlefront and enemy homeland, between uniformed combatants and civilian noncombatants. Bombing, it was believed, would destroy the enemy's ability and will to resist. That proved not to be the case.

In the 1920s some military strategists, including U.S. Gen. William "Billy" Mitchell, argued that air power would be a decisive weapon in future wars. When World War II broke out, the Germans were the first to use air power in a new way. They bombed enemy cities such as Warsaw, Rotterdam, and, by the fall of 1940, London. In London alone nearly 30,000 civilians lost their lives during the Battle of Britain.

It was the British who played the leading role in introducing strate-gic bombing to warfare. The Germans never equipped their air force with many heavy bombers. Their strategists thought mainly in terms of tactical bombing, which meant using medium bombers and fighters to provide support to armies in the field. British strategists, particularly Air Marshal Arthur "Bomber" Harris, argued for the systematic destruction of Germany's productive capacity, by means of attacks on its industrial centers. They believed such a strategy would in itself bring victory within reach. The first such attacks were launched in May 1940.

At first British bombers engaged in what was called "precision bombing," attempting to put their bombloads directly on top of factories, railroads, and similar targets. But the British bombed only at night, in the belief that they would lose fewer planes than in daylight raids. It was very difficult for bombers to hit precisely defined targets, so the British switched tactics. Their new tactic, "area bombing," called for dropping bombloads over a wide target area. Even if bombs did not land directly on top of a factory, fires set by the bombs might spread to it. Even if the factories were spared, the destruction of workers' housing in other parts of the city would, it was hoped, seriously damage German productivity. One early test of the new strategy came in May 1942 when Air Marshal Harris sent 1,046 planes to the German city of Cologne. This raid laid waste to 600 acres of the city and destroyed the homes of 45,000 residents.

The U.S. Air Force, which was not yet a separate branch of the military services, had only 26,000 men and 800 combat planes when the war broke out in 1939. The first airmen from the U.S. Army Air Force arrived in Britain in the spring of 1942, to set up what was designated the Eighth U.S. Air Force. Other air force commands would be set up later in the war in England, North Africa, and Italy, but the Eighth was always the most important U.S. unit. It grew to include 60 airbases spread across southeastern England, first under the command of Gen. Carl Spaatz, then in late 1942 under Gen. Ira Eaker. From 1944 until the end of the war, the Eighth Air Force was under Gen. James Doolittle, hero of the "Doolittle raid" on Tokyo. The once tiny U.S. Air Force grew to a mighty armada in the course of the war, including nearly 2.4 million men and some 80,000 planes in all theaters by 1945.

Unlike the British, the Americans decided to send their bombers over Europe during daytime. American bombers were equipped with the new Norden bombsight, allowing bombs to be dropped with greater accuracy from higher (and, theoretically, safer) altitudes. Americans, whose cities had not been bombed by German planes, were

Allied bombers over Europe *(National Archives)*

uncomfortable with the British tactic of area bombing. They hoped to spare civilian lives if they could. But the American planes faced heavy antiaircraft fire over targets that were often obscured by smoke or clouds. American daylight "precision" bombing was in reality not much more precise than British nighttime area bombing. The round-the-clock air raids, however, did prevent German defenders from ever being able to let their guard down. By August of 1942 American bombers were hitting targets in France; by January 1943 they began to bomb Germany itself.

Two heavy bombers provided the backbone of the U.S. Air Force in Europe. The B-17 Flying Fortress, so named for its heavy armament, was a four-engined plane that could cruise up to an altitude of 24,000 feet and had a maximum range of 1,850 miles. It could deliver up to 12,000 pounds of bombs, although on long-range missions a B-17 carried far less of a bombload to hold down on fuel consumption. The

B-24 Liberator had a longer range than the Flying Fortress, but it was unpopular with American air crews because it was less maneuverable at higher altitudes.

The 10-man crews of the bombers could expect to spend between five and 10 hours aloft on every mission. They wore oxygen masks and warm clothing to compensate for the thin, freezing air at high altitudes. Bombing crews were required to fly 25 combat missions before they were rotated to noncombat assignments. In some ways their lives were easier than those of the average combat GI, since they lived in comfortable barracks and could return to a hot shower and a good meal after a mission. But their losses were heavy. When they were dodging enemy fighters or antiaircraft fire ("flak") at 20,000 feet above enemy territory, few airmen felt especially privileged. An American war correspondent, Walter Cronkite, caught some of the sensation of aerial combat in his report of a February 1943 B-17 raid on the U-boat base at Wilhelmshaven, Germany. It was the first raid that war correspondents were allowed to accompany:

> The impressions of a first bombing mission are a hodge-podge of disconnected scenes like a poorly edited home movie—bombs falling past you from the formation above, a crippled bomber with smoke pouring from one motor limping along thousands of feet below, a tiny speck in the sky that grows closer and finally becomes an enemy fighter, a Focke-Wulf [a German fighter plane] peeling off above you somewhere and plummeting down, shooting its way through the formation; your bombardier pushing a button as calmly as if he were turning on a hall light, to send our bombs on the way.

When the Fortresses and Liberators first went into action, air force commanders hoped that they would be able to defend themselves with the heavy machine guns that poked out of the bombers' turrets. This was important, because, unfortunately, Allied fighter planes could not travel far enough to protect the bombers on raids deep inside Europe. German fighter pilots soon learned how to attack from angles that avoided the American bombers' defensive fire. The Germans began to take a heavy toll. In one ill-fated raid against the Axis oil refinery center in Ploesti, Romania, German fighters and antiaircraft fire shot down 53 of the 177 B-24s in the attack force. Many of the surviving planes were so badly damaged that they had to be scrapped. At that rate of loss, the entire U.S.

Air Force would have been eliminated in a few weeks. The effectiveness of German fighter attacks led to a suspension of American bombing raids on Germany until better protection could be provided.

The tide in the air war turned in 1944, after the conquest of southern Italy. Allied bombers began launching attacks on southern Germany from the Italian airbase at Foggia. German air defense had to be spread thinner to counter the new threat of assault from the south. By the summer of 1944 the Allies had overrun many of the Germans' advance warning stations in France. This meant that German fighters had less time to get in the air to head off Allied bombers coming from England. Most important of all, the U.S. Air Force was finally equipped with fighter planes capable of accompanying the bombers all the way to Germany and back.

The deadliest of the new American fighters was the P-51 Mustang, capable of making a 1,700-mile round trip and reaching top speeds of 440 miles per hour. It could outperform anything the *Luftwaffe* could throw against it. The first American bombing raid accompanied by Mustangs was launched on January 11, 1944. It met heavy resistance, and 60 out of a total of 663 bombers were shot down. But the 49 Mustangs accompanying the bombers shot down 15 German fighters without losing even one of their own planes. One experienced pilot, Maj. James Howard, single-handedly dove into a swarm of 30 German fighters attacking the American bombers. He shot down at least four and perhaps as many as six of the attackers, for which he was awarded the Congressional Medal of Honor.

The Allies were determined to win air superiority in the skies over France before the spring 1944 invasion. American bombers concentrated on German airplane factories and oil production facilities. They met with mixed success. German armaments minister Albert Speer was able to work miracles of production. He directed the rebuilding and expanding of Germany's factories, so that the production of German fighter planes actually increased in the course of the year. But the systematic attacks on oil refineries and storage facilities pinched fuel supplies for German planes and tanks.

Also, the dogfights in Germany's skies were taking their toll on German pilots. The *Luftwaffe* lost 1,000 planes in the first four months of 1944. Some of Germany's top aces met their end that spring. *Luftwaffe* Col. Egon Mayer, credited with 102 kills, was himself killed when his plane was shot down by a U.S. Thunderbolt in March 1944. Such expe-

Würzburg, Germany, after a heavy bombing, 1945 *(National Archives)*

rienced pilots could not be replaced. The payoff came on D day in 1944. Before the invasion General Eisenhower assured Allied troops, "If you see fighting aircraft over you, they will be ours." That was no idle boast. The Germans could mount only 300 sorties over all of France on June 6, while the Allies launched nearly 15,000.

During most of the spring and summer of 1944 the Allied air force was used in direct support of the invasion forces in France. They bombed German troops, tanks, supply dumps, and railroad facilities. In September 1944 the airmen turned their attention back to Germany. They launched an all-out offensive that would continue until mid-April

1945 when they ran out of targets to destroy. More than half of all bombs dropped on Germany fell during the last seven months of war.

At home, Americans were not always sure what to think of the strategy of bombing enemy cities. Almost without exception, Americans condemned the Germans for attacking civilians. In 1940 and 1941,

Albert Speer and German Industry under Allied Bombardment

ALBERT SPEER JOINED THE NAZI PARTY IN 1931, TWO years before Adolf Hitler came to power. He would prove himself one of Hitler's most able lieutenants. He first caught the *Führer's* eye as the architect who designed the vast assembly site where the Nazis held their annual mass rallies in Nuremberg, Germany. At Hitler's suggestion, Speer drew up plans (largely unrealized) to rebuild the German capital of Berlin in a grand monumental style. If his architectural designs were second-rate, he had real genius as an industrial manager, which he proved after he was appointed Reichminister for armaments and production by Hitler in 1942.

The Allied strategic bombing campaign was intended to cripple Germany's industrial might. But in fact, by coupling central planning with decentralized production, Speer was able to mobilize the entire Germany economy for waging total war. He also made extensive use of slave labor, drawn from Germany's concentration camps and saw to it that German workers were well fed on food requisitioned from the hungry populations of the countries Germany had occupied. Such tactics enabled Speer to increase German armament production steadily from 1942 until late in 1944. By January 1945 Speer, realizing that the war was lost, concentrated on protecting the remaining German factories from destruction at Hitler's orders. According to a postwar study prepared by the U.S. government, the *Wehrmacht* was "better equipped with weapons at the beginning of 1944" than it had been in mid-1941. Without Speer's efforts, the Nazis might have been forced to surrender months earlier.

At the postwar Nuremberg trials, Speer was tried for war crimes connected with his use of slave labor and sentenced to 20 years in prison. He was released from prison in 1966, published his memoirs soon afterward, and died in 1981.

OPERATIONAL RANGE OF U.S. ARMY AIR FORCES IN EUROPEAN AIR WAR, 1942–1945

pictures of London burning during the Battle of Britain had been one of the most effective arguments in favor of U.S. intervention. On the other hand, Americans also favored anything that would bring the war home to the enemy. For most of the war American armies were far from the homeland of Nazism. Bombing was a way of striking back when few other weapons were available. American leaders, and Hollywood movies like the 1943 film *Bombardier,* assured the public that Americans never intentionally bombed civilian targets.

The first doubts came with the destruction of the city of Dresden in eastern Germany by British and American bombers, in February 1945. Dresden, a beautiful and ancient city, was known for its production of porcelain dolls, not military weapons. British prime minister Churchill personally ordered its destruction. At least in part, the intention was to impress the Soviets (whose Red Army would soon conquer the city) of the destructive capabilities of Allied air power. Incendiaries dropped by British bombers set off a firestorm in Dresden that virtually leveled the city, killing 35,000 civilians.

All told, more than 400,000 German civilians lost their lives as a result of Allied bombing. But 79,265 Americans fliers and almost the same number of British fliers lost their lives in the air war over Europe. After the war, the United States sent experts to Germany to determine how effective the bombing campaign had been. The results were sobering. Strategic bombing, they concluded, did not break German civilian morale, as it was supposed to. Nor did it eliminate Germany's capacity to produce the weapons it needed to fight the war. German arms production remained adequate until the moment when Allied armies were already penetrating Germany's borders. When the Allies concentrated on targets like the oil refineries, they were able to obtain good results. When they indiscriminately destroyed whole cities, they achieved little except to make the war even more terrible than it need have been.

18

OPERATION OVERLORD

The invasion of Normandy was without question the most important battle fought in western Europe in World War II. The Allies' success in landing their troops and securing a beachhead on June 6, 1944, doomed Hitler. The landings at Anzio only a few months earlier had shown that success was by no means certain. Amphibious landings were inevitably extremely risky operations. Years of careful planning—and a certain amount of luck at the last moment—led to the Allied victory in Normandy.

It was a victory that Americans could claim a large role in bringing about. The invasion was commanded by an American, and American soldiers, sailors, and airmen made up a large proportion of the invading force. The invasion site had been decided by American insistence that this was the place to win the war against Hitler, finally forcing the British to abandon their Mediterranean-centered strategy. The ground fighting in North Africa, Sicily, and Italy, the battle against the U-boats in the Atlantic, and the air war over Germany and Nazi-occupied Europe—all were in preparation for the final great struggle that was to begin on the beaches and among the hedgerows of Normandy.

Allied strategists meeting in Washington in May 1943 set the date for the cross-channel invasion of France as May 1, 1944. In late November 1943 the so-called Big Three—Roosevelt, Churchill, and Stalin—met for their first wartime summit meeting in Tehran,

The Allied "Big Three"—Stalin, Roosevelt, and Churchill—hold their first wartime summit meeting, in Tehran, Iran, November 1943. *(Library of Congress)*

Iran. Churchill still had reservations about the planned invasion, but Roosevelt went ahead and pledged to Stalin that it would be launched the next spring. The Allies were now committed to the second front although due to a shortage of landing craft the invasion date would be postponed from May to June 1944.

The British preferred that one of their own generals command the invasion, code-named "Operation Overlord." However, because of the enormous contribution the Americans were making in men and material, they agreed to allow an American to take command. Dwight David "Ike" Eisenhower, who had proven his abilities in the invasions of North Africa, Sicily, and Italy, was appointed commander of Supreme Headquarters, Allied Expeditionary Force (SHAEF), in December 1943. Gen. Omar Bradley, brought in as Eisenhower's deputy in North Africa after the disaster at Kasserine Pass, was given command of U.S. Army forces scheduled to land in France. Bernard Montgomery, the hero of El Alamein, would be in command of British troops. On February 12, 1944, Eisenhower and his generals received momentous orders: "You will enter the continent of Europe and, in conjunction with the other

United Nations, undertake operations aimed at the heart of Germany and the destruction of her armed forces."

Planning for the invasion had been going on since 1942. The raid at Dieppe had provided an early and disastrous dress rehearsal. The fighting in North Africa, Sicily, and Italy had taught the Allies valuable lessons. If there was one lesson above all that the Allies had been forced to learn, it was not to underestimate the abilities of their enemy. Time and again the Germans had proven that, man for man and weapon for weapon, they fielded the world's toughest fighting force.

The Nazis had 60 divisions stationed in France under the command of Field Marshal Gerd von Rundstedt. Although of varying quality, their numbers included some of the best units in the German military. Hitler was determined that, when the invasion came, the Germans would hurl the Allies back into the sea. As he explained to his generals on March 18, 1944:

> Once defeated, the enemy will never try to invade again. Quite apart from their heavy losses they would need months to organize a fresh attempt. And an invasion failure would also deliver a crushing blow to British and American morale.

Field Marshal Rommel was sent to France in late 1943 to strengthen the "Atlantic Wall," the system of coastal fortifications that Hitler bragged would stop the Allies on the beaches. Rommel believed that everything depended on the first 24 hours after an invasion: "The war will be won or lost on the beaches." He put a half-million men to work constructing a network of bunkers, mine fields, barbed wire entanglements, and other obstacles along the Atlantic coast. Steel and wooden posts designed to rip the bottoms out of landing craft and gliders were put in place on the beaches and in inland meadows. These were known as "Rommel's asparagus."

The Allies had decided in July 1943 that the Cotentin peninsula of Normandy offered the best location for an invasion. The Germans, who had 3,000 miles of coastline to defend, did not know where the invasion would come. They put up the heaviest defenses in the Pas de Calais region of the French coast, where the channel dividing England and France was the narrowest. But the beaches on Normandy were not neglected.

Hitler personally believed that the invasion would come in Normandy. Uncharacteristically and unluckily for the Nazi cause, he did not impose his judgment on his generals. Rommel also believed that Normandy was the most likely site, but his commander in France, von Rundstedt, thought it would be the Pas de Calais. As a result, German defenders were spread between the two areas instead of concentrated in one. Rommel and von Rundstedt also disagreed on strategy. Rommel wanted to commit all forces to fight on the coast, while von Rundstedt wanted to retain reserves inland in case the Allies broke through. Hitler was not sure which of his generals to back. The lack of unity in the German command would prove a great weakness to them.

Allied strategists decided that in order to gain a foothold in France they would need to concentrate superior forces on a fairly narrow front. Then they would push inland as quickly as possible. The plans for the invasion went through many changes. In their final form they called for a combined assault from sea and air. Three airborne divisions (two American and one British) would land several miles inland to seize key strongholds and disrupt German communications and transportation. Six more divisions (three American, two British, and one Canadian) would land on a 60-mile-long beachhead between Caen and Cherbourg. All told, more than 150,000 men would be put ashore on D day, with hundreds of thousands more soon to follow.

By the spring of 1944, 3 million Allied soldiers, sailors, and airmen, plus 6 million tons of supplies, had been gathered in England in preparation for the invasion. Much of southern England was turned into a vast supply dump for Allied artillery, tanks, jeeps, ammunition, and food. Eisenhower joked, "Only the great number of barrage balloons floating constantly in British skies kept the islands from sinking under the waves." Never before in the history of warfare had such a huge and complex operation been staged. Everything had to be planned in advance, from how far offshore the destroyers should be stationed to fire on German coastal emplacements, to how to guarantee that each man going ashore was issued a package of chewing gum.

Part of the preparations for the invasion included an elaborate hoax, known as Operation Fortitude. A phony "First Army Group" was stationed near Dover in England, the most likely port to be used for an invasion of the Pas de Calais region. Allied radio operators broadcast a steady stream of fictitious orders to fool German eavesdroppers. Dummy tanks and landing craft were assembled on the ground to be spotted by German air reconnaissance flights. The Allies shot down reconnaissance planes that might have reported on the real invasion

Stars and Stripes
THE GI NEWSPAPER

AMERICANS ON THE HOME FRONT RELIED ON civilian newspaper and radio correspondents to tell them what was happening in the war. The soldiers at the front line relied on *Stars and Stripes,* the U.S. Army's own newspaper. *Stars and Stripes* first appeared during World War I but was shut down at the end of the war. In April 1942 it resumed publication, first as a weekly based in London and soon as a daily newspaper. Before the war ended, separate editions were being published in North Africa, Italy, France, and Hawaii, as well as the original London edition. *Stars and Stripes* was tremendously popular with its soldier-readers, because it was written by reporters who shared the hardships and dangers of the front line, and because it almost always took the viewpoint of the common GI in its reporting and other features. In addition to war news, the newspaper also carried sports, cartoons, and letters columns. One popular feature was the "B-Bag Column," which carried complaints from GIs under the motto "Blow it out here." But the newspaper's best-loved feature was almost certainly the "Willie and Joe" cartoons of Bill Mauldin, with their gritty appreciation of the sufferings of the combat infantryman. In a famous example, Willie and Joe are seated side by side on a muddy battlefield, and a grateful-looking Willie says to his comrade in arms: "Joe, yestiddy ya saved my life an' I swore I'd pay ya back. Here's my last pair of dry socks." Mauldin went on to a postwar career as a Pulitzer prize–winning cartoonist; *Stars and Stripes* remains in publication today as a newspaper for U.S. military forces stationed overseas.

---

preparations in other ports, but allowed those flying over Dover to return home unscathed. In the months of aerial bombardment that preceded the invasion, more bombs were dropped on the Pas de Calais area than on Normandy. As a result 19 German divisions were tied up guarding against invasion far from the actual site of the Allied landings.

In England the troops that would land on D day went through endless rehearsals for the invasion. For veterans of combat in North Africa, Sicily, and Italy, the training seemed like a waste of time. Those who had never seen combat tried to imagine what the real thing would be like. The civilian population of a 25-square-mile area of the coast of Devon in southwestern England was evacuated, to allow the Americans to stage war games with live ammunition. An unsought element of realism was added to the final rehearsal for the landings: German torpedo boats snuck into waters around the Allied flotilla and sunk two landing craft, drowning 700 Americans.

In late May 1944 the rehearsals came to an end. Soldiers were confined to their quarters, then shipped to "concentration areas" near ports and airfields from which they would depart. One Englishwoman who had married a jeep driver from the U.S. First Division recalled the last days of May 1944:

> As the tanks rumbled through the village streets, shaking the walls and windows, convoy upon convoy, we knew the invasion day was drawing nearer. We had about three weeks together. Bob's final overnight pass came and he walked down the street that morning after our goodbye and out of sight into the morning mist that was coming in from the sea. From then on they were confined to barracks and one morning a friend and myself walked up the hill to [his barracks] and they were gone.

Only when cut off from further contact with the outside world were the men briefed on their assignments. Even then, for security reasons they were not told their ultimate destination. When they were safely at sea they would finally be told that they were headed for Normandy.

There were a limited number of days each month when the tides and moon would be right for the requirements of an invasion by sea and air. If the Allies could not land sometime between June 5 and 7, they would have to postpone the attack until the end of the month. That would greatly increase the danger of the Germans learning of the invasion plans. On June 3, heavy rains were pelting England and France. The weather report was so unfavorable that Rommel left France for Germany to visit his wife on her birthday. In English ports and in the Channel men were already packed into landing craft. Early on the morning of June 4, Eisenhower, in his advance headquarters in Portsmouth, England, decided he had to postpone the invasion one day from June 5 to June 6. All that day he waited for a break in the weather. On the evening of June 4 Allied meteorologists forecast a break in the weather for June 6. There would be 36 hours of relatively good weather. That

U.S. Gen. Dwight D. Eisenhower talks with D day paratroops soon to be dropped behind enemy lines in France. *(National Archives)*

was just enough. At 9:45 P.M. on June 4 Eisenhower gave the order for the attack to go forward on June 6. "I don't like it, but there it is," he said. "I don't see how we can possibly do anything else." German meteorologists, lacking Atlantic weather stations, still thought the bad weather would hold another few days.

By the end of the day of June 5, more than 2,500 ships carrying the Allied invasion force were heading toward the Normandy coast. More than 1,000 planes and gliders were being readied on English airfields to carry the airborne troops into battle. Every man who boarded a ship or a plane for Europe was given a letter from Eisenhower with his order of the day:

> You are about to embark on a great crusade, toward which we have striven these many months . . . The tide has turned. The free men of the world are marching together to victory . . .

Eisenhower had one last task to perform. He scribbled down the note he would release to the world if the invasion failed:

The troops, the air and navy did all that bravery and devotion to duty could do. If any blame or fault attaches to the attempt it is mine alone.

He did not have to use the note.

19
D DAY

Nothing went quite the way the Allies had planned on D day, June 6, 1944. Paratroopers were dropped miles from the right drop zone. Bombers missed their targets. Landing craft were launched too far out and deposited troops on the wrong beaches. Amphibious tanks filled with water and sank to the bottom of the sea. Fortunately, in war both sides make mistakes. The German high command responded to the invasion with paralyzing indecision. German commanders in the field were often confused and unprepared for the challenge confronting them. Courage, luck, and improvisation helped the Allies survive their own mistakes. By the evening of June 6 they were back on the European continent to stay.

General Eisenhower spent a nervous day as the Allied invasion armada sailed across the stormy English Channel on June 5. In the evening he drove to several airbases in England, where the paratroopers of the U.S. 101st ("Screaming Eagles") Airborne and Eighty-second ("All American") Airborne were getting ready to take off for France. He spent a few hours with the soldiers, making small talk, asking them where they were from, and wishing them good luck.

The paratroopers went into battle heavily weighed down with gear. Since they would be dropped miles behind enemy lines, to seize key bridges and road intersections on the east and west flanks of the invasion zone, they had to carry with them everything they would need in two or three days of fighting. That meant, in addition to their weapons, they had to carry extra rations and ammunition, grenades, dynamite, and land mines. Some carried bazookas and small mortars, so that they

D day, June 6, 1944: U.S. Coast Guard landing craft head for the Normandy coast. Barrage balloons are for protection against low-flying strafing planes. *(National Archives)*

would have some way of protecting themselves against German panzers. Each paratrooper carried a knife in his boot, in case he had to cut himself loose quickly from his parachute when he landed.

The planes, most of them twin-engined Douglas C-47 transports, took off from England around 11 P.M. on June 5. It was a two- to three-hour flight to carry 13,000 men from the U.S. Eighty-second and 101st Airborne and the British Sixth Airborne to their assigned jump zones. The paratroopers smoked or slept or were silent with their own thoughts as the hundreds of planes flying in V formations passed over the huge invasion armada on the seas below. All went well until they reached the coast of Normandy. There the planes carrying the Americans ran into a huge cloud bank and trouble. Many of the pilots were inexperienced. The combination of clouds and, in some cases, German antiaircraft fire, threw them way off course. As the "sticks" of American paratroopers jumped (each planeload of 18 men was called a "stick") they drifted down over unfamiliar territory. Often they became widely separated from the other men in their units. A few landed right on target, but some wound up as far as 35 miles away from where they were supposed to be.

On the ground, officers tried to gather up men in the area and figure out how to get to their assigned targets. Some of the men did not survive the jump, landing in trees or drowning in the river valleys that the Germans had deliberately flooded. Many of the radios the paratroopers carried with them were lost or damaged in the drop. Yet somehow, in all the confusion, small groups of men got organized and set off to accomplish their missions.

The Germans were slow to react to the airborne landings. Field Marshal von Rundstedt was alerted at his headquarters, but he decided that the attack in Normandy was only a diversionary attack. He believed it was intended to distract the Germans from the real invasion, which would come in the Pas de Calais area. (The Allies did what they could to encourage that belief by dropping loads of dummy paratroopers in

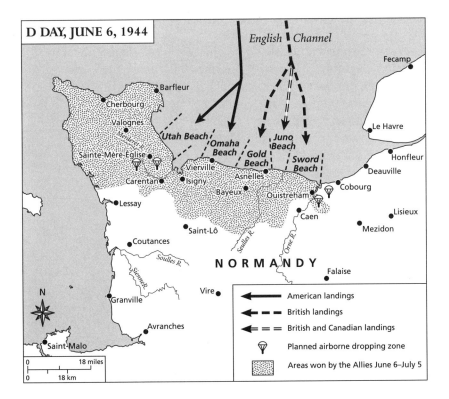

the Pas de Calais.) Von Rundstedt delayed sending in his panzer reserves to Normandy, although he finally decided to do so. Other reserve forces in France were under Hitler's direct command and could not be moved without his permission. But when von Rundstedt contacted Hitler's headquarters in the middle of the night with news of the Allied drops, Hitler's aides refused to wake him up. The führer needed his sleep.

Even on the battlefront, the Germans did not seem to realize what was happening. Many regimental officers had gone to the French city of Rennes for a staff meeting (to discuss plans to counter the invasion, ironically). Among those sent to Rennes was the commander of the German division defending the town of Ste.-Mère-Église, which sat along a militarily important highway. His absence would be missed. German soldiers in Ste.-Mère-Église were awakened by the initial parachute drop and shot many paratroopers from the Eighty-second Airborne as they descended. Then, amazingly, they went back to bed. When the Americans returned in force a few hours later, they took the town without difficulty, capturing 30 Germans in their beds.

The French Resistance had been alerted to the launching of the invasion by a coded message sent by the BBC (the British radio network). They cut telephone and telegraph wires. Some German units were cut off from communications with their headquarters. Others ignored the sounds of battle around them. Sgt. Harrison Summers of the 101st Airborne learned this when he launched what was virtually a one-man assault on a German barracks. He burst into building after building, gunning down the Germans inside. This had been going on for some time when Summers kicked in the door of another building and found 15 German soldiers calmly eating their breakfasts. Their strange lack of concern for the noise outside cost them their lives.

The American and British paratroopers were fighting desperate battles inland for control of the bridges and roads the Germans would need to send in reinforcements. Meanwhile, the invasion armada approached the coast of Normandy. With the bad weather in the English Channel, German naval and aerial reconnaissance had been relaxed. The Allied fleet approached the coast unnoticed. The invasion force was divided into five convoys, each headed for a separate beach. The Americans would land on the westernmost beaches: the U.S. Fourth Infantry Division on Utah Beach, the U.S. First Infantry Division and Twenty-ninth Infantry Division on Omaha Beach. British soldiers landed on Gold and Sword Beaches, and the Canadians landed on Juno Beach.

American invasion forces wade through the surf toward Omaha Beach on the Normandy coast, June 6, 1944. *(Library of Congress)*

In the early morning hours, soldiers scheduled to go in with the first wave climbed down cargo netting from the sides of the troop transports into a variety of smaller landing craft. Photographer Robert Capa, who would take some of the most famous photographs of the war in the next few hours, went in with the first wave on a landing craft headed for Omaha Beach. The men had been fed a big breakfast aboard the transport ships. That proved to have been a mistake as they rode for three hours through choppy seas. Capa wrote:

> In no time, the men started to puke. But this was a polite as well as a carefully prepared invasion, and little paper bags had been provided for the purpose.

Seasickness would soon prove the least of their problems. When they reached Omaha Beach at H-hour, 6:30 A.M., they discovered that the preliminary naval bombardment had done little to destroy German defenses. The bombers were supposed to have left the beach cratered with deep sheltering holes. They had missed the beaches entirely, dropping their loads farther inland. When Capa jumped out of the landing craft, he found himself under heavy fire:

> The water was cold, and the beach still more than a hundred yards away. The bullets tore holes in the water around me, and I made for the nearest steel obstacle. A soldier got there at the same time, and for a few minutes we shared its cover. He took the waterproofing off his rifle and began to shoot without much aiming at the smoke-hidden beach. The sound of his rifle gave him enough courage to move forward and he left the obstacle to me. It was a foot larger now, and I felt safe enough to take pictures of the other guys hiding just like I was.

Along the coast to the west, on Utah Beach, the Americans met relatively light resistance. Although the American landing craft put the first wave of soldiers on Utah about 2,000 yards south of where they were supposed to be, the soldiers quickly gained their objectives. The German defenses were manned by second-rate troops who had been hard hit by both naval shelling and bombing. Most of the Allies' new amphibious tanks designed for the invasion had made it to the beach intact. They proved a great help to the infantry, who were moving inland within an hour after the initial landing. By midday they had linked up with paratroopers from the 101st Airborne. The British and Canadian soldiers on Gold, Juno, and Sword Beaches enjoyed similar success.

On Omaha Beach the situation remained serious. Undetected by Allied intelligence, crack German units had moved in to take over the coastal defenses weeks earlier. They raked the beaches with heavy artillery and machine-gun fire. The American amphibious tanks off Omaha were swamped in heavy seas; 27 of 29 tanks that were supposed to land on one section of the beach sank before reaching shore. Soldiers huddled in the water behind anti–landing craft obstacles, preventing engineers from the Sixth Special Engineer Brigade from blowing up the obstacles as planned. Each new wave of Americans piled up behind the last. The beach was littered with wrecked vehicles, landing craft, dead bodies, and discarded weapons.

Some soldiers made it across the exposed sand to a low concrete seawall at the end of the beach. The wall offered a little protection from German guns. There they huddled, unable to go any farther. Medics did

Landing Craft

THE WINNING WEAPON IN AMPHIBIOUS WARFARE

AMONG THE MOST FAMILIAR IMAGES OF WORLD WAR II are photographs depicting U.S. Marines storming ashore on Pacific islands such as Iwo Jima and soldiers landing under heavy fire on D day in the Normandy invasion. Amphibious warfare, the delivery of armed forces from shipboard to a hostile shoreline, was nothing new in U.S. military history; American fighting men had splashed ashore in the 19th century, in conflicts ranging from the U.S.-Mexican War to the Spanish-American War.

What was new in World War II was the development of specialized landing craft designed to get Allied forces safely ashore, in sufficient numbers and with the weapons, equipment, and vehicles they needed to destroy resistance on the beaches. Barges and rowboats, the traditional means of bringing troops ashore, would never have worked against an entrenched enemy equipped with machine guns and heavy artillery zeroed in on the landing zone.

Andrew Higgins, a New Orleans shipbuilder, built tens of thousands of modern landing vessels for the U.S. Navy, including the 36-foot-long flat-bottomed boat he personally designed. This boat, known as the Landing Craft Vehicle and Personnel (LCVP) and commonly called a "Higgins Boat," could carry a platoon of soldiers directly onto a hostile beach. Higgins's shipyard workers also built larger vessels, capable of delivering tanks and other vehicles, as well as troops, including the British-designed Landing Craft Tank (LCT) and the Landing Ship Tank (LST). The latter vessel was so large that it could cross the ocean on its own steam, with dozens of vehicles crammed into its hold, but it was shallow-bottomed enough to pull right up onto an invasion beach to discharge its cargo. General Eisenhower thought so highly of these vessels that he once said of Higgins, "He is the man who won the war for us."

what they could to help the many wounded men, bandaging their wounds and giving them shots of morphine. From his command post on a battleship at sea, Gen. Omar Bradley received a steady stream of bad news from Omaha Beach. Around noon he was considering

Allied invasion forces faced such formidable defenses as this monster Nazi gun battery, with walls 13 feet thick shielding four cannon of 10 1/4-inch bore. *(National Archives)*

diverting the remaining troops scheduled to go in there to Utah Beach instead.

By then, however, scattered groups of Americans had ventured out from the shelter of the seawall and fought their way up to the bluffs above the beach. Col. George Taylor of the First Division rallied his men by telling them, "The only people on the beach are the dead and those who are going to die—now let's get the hell out of here." Navy destroyers helped by moving in closer to shore than planned and directing deadly fire on German pillboxes. The situation remained extremely risky, with the beachhead extended no more than a mile and a half inland as night fell. Fortunately no German counterattack came to drive the Americans back into the sea. More and more troops moved up off the beach into the villages beyond. Landing craft began to remove the wounded for the long trip back to hospitals in England.

Some of the hardest fighting that day took place west of Omaha Beach. Specially trained U.S. Rangers assaulted a German gun battery atop a 100-foot-high cliff known as Pointe du Hoc. Half the Ranger force never made it to the right beach. Either their landing craft were blown up on the way in or the current carried them far down the beach away from the cliffs. But about 200 Rangers made it to the beach below the cliff. They fired rockets with grappling hooks and ropes to the cliff top, then pulled and fought their way up. The Germans shot at them, tried to cut their ropes, and dropped hand grenades down on them. Still they kept coming. When they made it over the top, they killed all the Germans within reach. Then they looked for the guns, which it turned out had never been mounted in place. Once they destroyed the guns, which were hidden nearby, they could do nothing else for the invasion but hold on. For the next two days they held out against repeated counterattacks. All but 90 of the Rangers were dead or wounded when they were finally relieved.

While the battles raged along the ocean front, Hitler slept on undisturbed. When he awoke in the late morning, he was briefed on the invasion but seemed unconcerned. He had convinced himself that what was going on in Normandy was not the main Allied attack. It was not until

A Coast Guard combat photographer came upon this memorial to a dead American soldier somewhere on the shell-blasted shore of Normandy. *(National Archives)*

3:30 in the afternoon of June 6 that he authorized the release of the SS panzer divisions being held in reserve in France. It was too late to make any difference to the German cause on D day.

By the end of the day on June 6, 1944, more than 150,000 Allied troops had landed, capturing 80 square miles of Normandy. The cost had been heavy on Omaha Beach, where more than 1,000 Americans had died. On Utah, less than 200 Americans lost their lives. The next day, while German artillery still hammered the beaches, Allied engineers began constructing the "Mulberries," or artificial harbors. These would provide the port of entry for hundreds of thousands more troops and tons of supplies in the next few weeks. Within four days, all five invasion beaches were linked together, no longer at risk from German counterattack. The Allies' great gamble had paid off. The liberation of Europe had begun.

20

THE LIBERATING ARMY

In the German blitzkrieg in the spring of 1940, France had been conquered in less than three weeks. The Allied forces landing in France in June 1944 gained a somewhat slower but still impressive victory. In less than three months, they liberated Paris; in only five months they cleared the Germans from almost all of France, Luxembourg, Belgium, and part of Holland. The U.S. Army had come a long way from the days in North Africa when it was an untried and poorly led fighting force. The Germans would strike back with everything they had in December 1944, but battle-hardened Americans proved up to the challenge in the Battle of the Bulge.

The Allies wasted no time in expanding the beachhead they established in Normandy on June 6. While British forces under General Montgomery fought to capture the city of Caen to the east of the invasion beaches, American forces were assigned to capture the port of Cherbourg on the northern coast of the Cotentin Peninsula. Gen. Joseph Lawton "Lightning Joe" Collins, a veteran of the Guadalcanal fighting, led the attack on Cherbourg, which fell to the Americans on June 27. Cherbourg's capture gave the Allies a desperately needed port, for the artificial Mulberry harbors they had constructed off the invasion beaches had limited capacity. Moreover, they were destroyed by storms in late June. By early September troop convoys from the United States were unloading directly in Cherbourg rather than having to stop off first in England for reshipment to France.

By July 10 the strategic city of Caen was also captured. The Allies were now in a position to break out of Normandy into the rest of France. By a month after D day almost 1 million Allied soldiers were crowded into Normandy. American forces in France were reorganized in July. Gen. Courtney Hodges was placed in command of the U.S. First Army, and Gen. George Patton (in his first combat command since the Sicily campaign) was given command of the U.S. Third Army. Both armies were under the overall command of Gen. Omar Bradley. Allied generals were eager to move out of Normandy, a region of narrow roads and high hedgerows (earthen and brush barriers fencing off farmers' fields). German snipers and machine gunners offered stiff resistance from behind the cover of the hedgerows and from within Normandy's stone farmhouses. Some feared that the fighting in Normandy would turn into First World War–style trench warfare.

At the end of July American troops launched Operation Cobra to break out from Saint-Lô, a city south of the invasion beaches. The war in France suddenly became a war of rapid movement. The German Seventh Army, facing the Americans at Saint-Lô, was weakened from weeks

Equipped with an improvised plow, an Allied "tank-dozer" smashes through a Normandy hedgerow that was used for protection by fleeing Germans. *(National Archives)*

of hard fighting. Hitler ordered his troops not to retreat, but refused to move reserves from the Pas de Calais to Normandy, still deceived by the phony invasion preparations in Dover. The American offensive at Saint-Lô opened with an attack by more than 1,000 Allied bombers, which dropped their bombloads so densely that it was called "carpet bombing." (Some of the bombs went astray, killing 131 Americans on July 24 and 25, including Gen. Leslie McNair. This led some GIs to make bitter jokes about the "American *Luftwaffe*.") But the bombing stunned the German defenders, opening the way for the American breakthrough.

American tanks raced into the neighboring coastal region of Brittany, making 40-mile advances some days. The Americans would soon liberate all of the province except the two ports at Lorient and Saint-Nazaire. (These remained in German hands until May 1945, cut off and useless to the Nazis.) The U.S. Third Army, under General Patton, now swung east toward the Seine River and Paris.

At Hitler's insistence the German Seventh Army counterattacked on August 7. Outnumbered, outgunned, and faced with absolute Allied air superiority, the Germans fell into a trap, surrounded on three sides by American forces. When British troops failed to move quickly enough to shut off their exit, some 35,000 Germans escaped through the "Falaise gap." On August 19 the trap was finally closed. When the battle ended, 50,000 Germans had been captured and 10,000 killed in the "Falaise pocket." Between June 6 and the end of August, the Germans had suffered a half-million casualties, including more than 200,000 soldiers taken prisoner.

Nazi Germany's future looked increasingly grim. The Germans were caught in a vise between the Allies pushing eastward in France, and the Russians pushing westward through Poland, Hungary, Romania, and Yugoslavia. Hitler still had hopes for victory, launching his "vengeance weapons" in the summer of 1944. Starting a week after the Normandy invasion, V-1 bombs (small, pilotless planes carrying explosive charges) began to rain down on London from launching pads in northern France. These were followed in August by V-2 rockets carrying one-ton warheads. Hitler's high hopes for his new secret weapons were fantasies. Neither the V-1 nor the V-2 did anything to slow the Allied advance, although they did kill thousands of civilians.

Many of Hitler's generals were convinced that the war was lost no matter what Germany did. A group of high-ranking German officers plotted to assassinate Hitler, seize control of the government, and open peace negotiations. On July 20 they exploded a bomb in a conference room in Hitler's "Wolf's Lair" headquarters in East Prussia. Hitler suffered only minor wounds from the explosion. Soon the Gestapo arrested, tortured, and executed thousands of people suspected of being involved in the plot. One of the victims of this purge was Field Marshal Rommel, who was in Germany recovering from wounds suffered when a British fighter strafed his car in France. Rommel had not played an active role in the conspiracy against Hitler, but he had known about it beforehand. He was now given the choice of committing suicide or being arrested. To spare his family, he swallowed cyanide. The Nazis announced that he had died of his Normandy wounds and gave him a hero's funeral.

In August the noose around Hitler's neck was drawn still tighter with the landing of another American army in France. Despite British objections, the U.S. Seventh Army under the command of Gen. Alexander Patch landed on France's southern coast on the Mediterranean, between Cannes and Toulon. The operation was supposed to have taken place in June, but the landings at Anzio the previous winter had taken away the landing craft set aside for the French operation. Churchill, thinking about the postwar settlement, had wanted Allied forces in Italy to push on into Hungary and Austria before the Soviet Red Army got there. The United States insisted that military rather than postwar political considerations should determine strategy; all available Allied resources should be concentrated on the main drive through France to Germany. Allied forces soon captured Marseilles, opening another port for the Allies. The U.S. Seventh Army made a rapid advance northward through France, linking up with the U.S. Third Army on September 12.

After the disaster of the Falaise pocket, German resistance in western France had crumbled. Patton's Third Army raced eastward toward Paris. At first the Americans intended to bypass the city. But when the French Resistance launched an uprising against the German garrison in Paris, the Allies were forced to change their plans. On August 25 a Free French division aided by the U.S. Fourth Division rolled into the city. The German commander and his garrison surrendered after a brief fight, ignoring Hitler's orders to destroy the city. On August 26 a crowd of 2 million Parisians cheered Gen. Charles de Gaulle, leader of the Free French cause, as he led a parade of Allied troops and tanks down the Champs-Élysées in the center of Paris.

Allied troops' victory parade down the boulevard Champs-Élysées in liberated Paris. *(National Archives)*

By September the Allied advance had proceeded much farther than had been expected in the preinvasion timetable. The Belgian port of Antwerp fell to the British on September 4, although German forces still held the river approaches leading into the port. Most of Belgium and Luxembourg were liberated by mid-September, while the battered remnants of the German armies in France were being pushed steadily back toward Germany.

Allied generals now expected the war to be over in a few months and debated which strategy would bring victory the quickest. General Montgomery argued that the Allied advance should be made along a narrow front, pushing north through Belgium and Holland to encircle the Ruhr industrial region of Germany. General Eisenhower favored a broad front with several Allied armies pushing simultaneously northward and eastward. A compromise was ultimately agreed to. The Americans in France would continue to push eastward toward the Rhine, but priority in supplies would be given to Montgomery's forces pushing northward. The Allied armies suffered from serious supply problems by this time, finding it particularly hard to provide enough fuel to their fast-moving tanks. These problems were not solved until late November, when the approaches to Antwerp were secured for Allied shipping.

To carry out Montgomery's planned advance, the Allies launched Operation Market Garden in mid-September. This was a combined air and ground assault to capture key bridges over rivers and canals in Holland. The goal was to open up the road for the Allied attack on Germany from the north. On September 17 American and British paratroopers landed in Holland. The Americans captured their objectives without

Churchill and Eisenhower *(U.S. Army)*

much difficulty, but the British paratroopers at Arnhem, the farthest bridge from the Allied lines, ran into trouble. Cut off from reinforcement, the paratroopers were unable to hold the bridge against German counterattack. Only 2,400 of the 10,000 who landed at Arnhem were able to make their way back to Allied lines.

Meanwhile the U.S. First, Third, and Seventh Armies continued to drive Germans back toward their own borders. In early October the U.S. First Army cracked the "West Wall," the defensive line running along the German border. On October 21 the Americans captured the city of Aachen, just across the Belgian-German border, the first German territory captured by the Allies.

To the South, Allied armies were poised at the brink of entering Germany. The U.S. Third Army breached Hitler's West Wall by seizing crossings over the Saar River on November 24, while the U.S. Seventh Army was approaching Germany's border through the Vosges Mountains. On the eastern front the Russians captured a first foothold in German East Prussia in October. The Allied offensive slowed down in early December because of rough terrain, bad weather, and stiffening German resistance. But time was fast running out for Hitler's Third Reich.

Hitler had one more trick up his sleeve. By stripping the eastern front of troops and tanks, he gathered together a striking force of 24 divisions. Maintaining absolute radio silence, the Germans massed their forces behind the German-Belgian border without discovery by Allied intelligence. Hitler's plan was to strike westward through the rugged Ardennes Forest, which had been left lightly guarded by the Allies. He hoped to drive a wedge through the British and American armies, and then to recapture Antwerp. A major Allied defeat, Hitler hoped, would end the threat from the west. This would allow him to concentrate on defending Germany's eastern border from the Soviets.

The German attack on December 16 came as a total surprise. The outnumbered Americans were driven back in confusion. The attack was aided by the infiltration into American lines of English-speaking German soldiers in American uniforms who cut telephone lines and killed isolated American soldiers. The GIs soon did not know who they could trust. At roadblocks soldiers were quizzed about sports and Hollywood gossip to see if they were really Americans. The massacre of 86 captured Americans by SS troops at Malmedy, Belgium, spread fear and anger in the American lines.

Under cloudy skies that kept Allied planes from hitting back, the Germans were able to advance 15 miles in the first two days. Eventually they created a bulge in Allied lines 65 miles deep and 45 miles wide—which is how the episode came to be known as the Battle of the Bulge. They might have penetrated much farther had it not been for the stubborn American defense of the Belgian city of Bastogne, located at an important road junction.

The U.S. 101st Airborne had been rushed to Bastogne after the start of the German offensive. By December 21 Bastogne was surrounded.

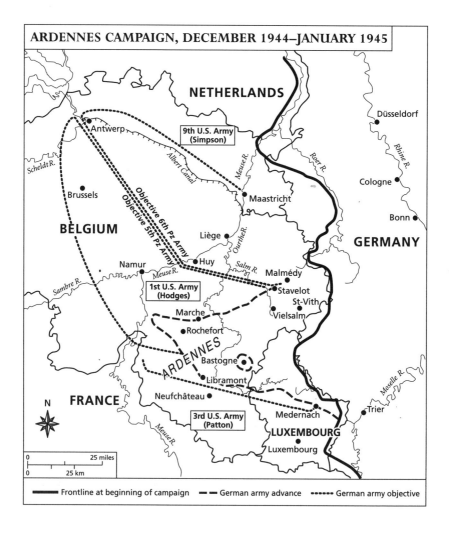

ARDENNES CAMPAIGN, DECEMBER 1944–JANUARY 1945

"Repple Depple"

INFANTRY REPLACEMENTS IN ITALY AND FRANCE

IN THE FIRST TWO YEARS OF WORLD WAR II AMERICAN soldiers went overseas to fight alongside men they already knew. The U.S. Army expanded dramatically in those years, to a total of 90 divisions (roughly 15,000 men to a division). These men had trained together and would fight together. It was the kind of experience that welded them, in the words of historian Stephen Ambrose, into a "band of brothers." But in the fierce fighting of 1944–45, with the U.S. Army sustaining heavy casualties in Italy and France, there were no more new divisions available to move up to the front lines. Instead, the army chose to send individual replacements into already existing frontline divisions, to take the place of those killed or severely wounded in combat. In theory, it seemed like a good idea, for the new men would be able to learn from the experience of combat veterans. In practice, things did not work out so well.

Starting in July 1944, the U.S. Army was short of riflemen in Europe. Casualties had been and would continue to be heavier than expected. Replacements rushed to Europe and deposited in huge replacement depot camps in Italy and France (known in GI slang as "repple depples"), were parceled out as needed to frontline units. They were often undertrained, unfamiliar with the weapons they were handed, and with none of the ingrained skills and habits needed to survive for long on the front lines. Veterans, figuring the replacements would soon be dead, did not want to get to know them and did not pass on the wisdom of their hard-won combat experience. Nonetheless, by the time the Battle of the Bulge had ended in January 1945, a majority of U.S. combat infantrymen in Europe were replacements.

The outnumbered Americans, fighting in snow and freezing rain, were battered by German 88s and Tiger tanks. They were also running out of ammunition, and until the weather cleared had no hope of resupply from the air. On December 22, the Germans demanded the surrender of the city. Gen. Anthony McAuliffe responded with a single word: "Nuts."

On December 23 the skies above Bastogne cleared and 250 planes dropped bundles of ammunition to the defenders of the city. On Christ-

German prisoners captured during the Battle of the Bulge
(National Archives)

mas Day there was house-to-house fighting in Bastogne as the Germans launched an all-out assault. The walking wounded in the American hospital were given rifles and sent out to help in the battle. They held the line.

The next afternoon three tanks from Patton's Third Army broke through German lines and reached Bastogne. More would soon follow. The siege was over, and so was the German offensive. It was not until January, however, that the German lines were rolled back to where they had been before the start of the Bulge campaign. Captured German documents after the war revealed that in the Battle of the Bulge the Germans finally came to respect American fighting capabilities. According to a German military report in January 1945, the American soldier was a "first-rate, well trained, and often physically superior opponent." Hitler's last gamble had cost the Germans 120,000 killed, wounded, and captured; the Americans suffered 76,800 casualties.

A lot of men died so that Adolf Hitler could live a few more weeks. But final defeat could only be postponed; the days of Nazi conquest were over. In the spring of 1945 the Allied armies moved into Germany for the kill.

21
VICTORY
OVER NAZISM

When Hitler came to power in the spring of 1933 he had boasted that his "new order" in Germany would last 1,000 years. Twelve years later his "Thousand Year Reich" lay in ruins, its cities reduced to rubble, its armies in defeat, its population homeless and hungry. As the Allied armies swept through Germany in the spring of 1945 they came both as conquerors and liberators. In places with names like Dachau and Buchenwald they uncovered evidence of the full, monstrous evil of Nazism. And when victorious American and Soviet soldiers linked up in April 1945, it seemed as if the world was ready to do away with the horror of war forever.

The Allied armies still faced some hard fighting at the start of the new year in January 1945. The Germans launched a miniature version of the Battle of the Bulge on December 31 from the so-called Colmar pocket, their last major stronghold on the western side of the Rhine. Although the attack caused the Americans some anxious moments, the Germans were stopped along the Moder River by the U.S. Seventh Army. The Colmar pocket was wiped out by early February.

From that point on, the Allies never lost the initiative. On the eastern front the Red Army had launched its final great offensive on January 12, seizing Warsaw on January 17, crossing the Polish-German border on January 30, capturing Vienna on April 13, and surrounding Berlin on April 25. From the west, British and Canadian forces along with the U.S. Ninth Army attacked the Rhineland. By March 13 they

Crossing the Rhine under enemy fire at Saint Goar, March 1945
(National Archives)

had wiped out all German resistance west of the Rhine. As the Germans fell back, they prepared to make their last stand along the eastern bank of the Rhine River, swollen by winter rains. If they could destroy all of its bridges, the Germans hoped to hold the Allies at the river, the way they had in Italy a year earlier, at the Rapido.

The U.S. First Army had captured the city of Cologne on the west bank of the Rhine on March 7. That same day the Americans found an unexpected prize farther south along the river. An American patrol, entering the town of Remagen, learned from a German prisoner that the bridge still spanning the Rhine was due to blow up in 45 minutes. Sgt. Alexander Drabik led a platoon down to the bridge and captured it in the face of heavy enemy fire. The explosives the Germans had rigged damaged but failed to destroy the bridge. By midnight nine American tanks had crossed over the Rhine to establish a bridgehead on its eastern shore. Army engineers quickly repaired the damage to the bridge, and by the next day more than 8,000 Americans were across the Rhine. Hitler was so infuriated that he had four German officers executed for allowing the bridge to be captured intact. The bridge at Remagen finally

Axis POWs in the United States

BY THE END OF THE WAR, CLOSE TO 2 MILLION GER-
man prisoners of war (POWs) were in the custody of the U.S. Army.
Most of these surrendered in the final weeks of the war and were held
in prison camps in Germany. But hundreds of thousands of enemy soldiers had been captured earlier in the war: in North Africa, Sicily and
Italy, and France. Of these, 325,000 Germans and 50,000 Italians were
sent to the United States, where they were held in more than 500 POW
camps spread across the country. There were also about 5,000 Japanese POWs sent to the United States—their numbers were small because
the Japanese rarely allowed themselves to be captured alive. Captured
enlisted men were put to work harvesting crops and in other jobs that
allowed American manpower to be freed up for war work. POW officials tried to separate the hardcore Nazis from ordinary German soldiers, and there were few problems in maintaining security. Many
POWs were just happy to be sitting out the rest of the war in safety
and comparative comfort. Although more than 1,000 German POWs
managed to escape from POW camps in the United States during the
war, few made it all the way back to Germany. There is no question
that Axis prisoners who fell into the hands of the Americans were far
luckier than those captured on the eastern front by the Red Army. The
Russians put their prisoners to hard labor in rebuilding the devastated
Soviet Union, and many hundreds of thousands of them died while in
captivity. The last POWs in the United States were returned to their
home countries by the summer of 1946; it was not until the mid-1950s
that the last German prisoners in the Soviet Union were released.

collapsed on March 17 from heavy use. By that time, however, the Allies
had constructed 62 additional bridges across the Rhine.

The Allies now kept up unrelenting pressure on the Germans. The
Canadians drove northward to cut off the Germans in the Netherlands.
The British moved out along the North German Plain. The U.S. Ninth
Army and the U.S. First Army encircled the Germans in the Ruhr industrial district, closing their trap on April 1. More than 300,000 Germans
were surrounded. Their commander, Field Marshal Walther Model,
committed suicide. One after another, German cities fell to the Allies.

U.S. forces captured Mannheim on March 19, and Nuremberg and Munich on April 30. Patton's Third Army tanks raced along the autobahn (superhighway) system the Nazis had built, reaching the Czechoslovakian frontier on April 23. Long lines of disarmed and demoralized German prisoners trudged westward, guarded by Sherman tanks, to huge prisoner-of-war camps.

Allied forces in Italy also resumed the offensive. Gen. Karl Wolff, commander of SS forces in Italy, had contacted American OSS agents in Switzerland in February. He was trying to arrange for the surrender of the German armies in Italy. The Russians, however, denounced the contacts between Wolff and the OSS. They feared that the Allies might still try to make a separate peace with the Nazis. In April the British Eighth Army and the U.S. Seventh Army broke through the last of the Gothic line defenses into the Po Valley plain. Italian partisans rose up in a general revolt, capturing Genoa, Milan, and Turin from the Germans before the Allies could reach the cities. Allied armies cut off the Germans from retreat to the Alps, and on May 2 the German army in Italy surrendered.

As the German armies retreated, the horrors of Hitler's secret "Final Solution" were revealed to the world. World War II had provided the Nazis the opportunity they sought to impose their vision of "racial purity" on Europe. Jews, Gypsies, and other "non-Aryans" were rounded up and murdered in the millions. Before they were through, the Nazis killed some 11 million civilians, 6 million of them Jews. At first the Nazis shot their victims and buried them in mass graves. By 1941 they had set up a system of death camps in Poland, where thousands could be gassed to death every day and their bodies burned in giant ovens. Trains from all over occupied Europe were soon pulling into camps such as Auschwitz, Treblinka, and Majdanek, carrying millions of men, women, and children to their deaths. Millions more worked as slave laborers under inhuman conditions in Nazi war industries.

Rumors of the death camps had reached the outside world as early as 1942. It was not until the spring of 1945, however, when the Allied armies began liberating concentration camps in Germany, that the full horror of what had taken place sank in. The camps in Germany had not originally been set up as death camps. Dachau and Buchenwald were built in the 1930s to hold political prisoners; during the war they became transport centers for slave laborers. But as the Russians overran the sites of Polish camps like Auschwitz, the inmates who had not

VICTORY OVER NAZISM

Slave laborers found in their tomblike bunks in Buchenwald, one of the most notorious German concentration camps *(National Archives)*

already been murdered were marched westward to camps in Germany. There the Germans starved and murdered them as quickly as they could, trying to complete the Final Solution and cover up the evidence before the Allies could arrive.

The end came too quickly for the Nazis to succeed. American soldiers captured the slave labor camps at Ohrdurf on April 5, and at Nordhausen-Dora on April 6. They liberated Buchenwald on April 11, Dachau on April 19, and Mauthausen on May 5. Everywhere they found heaps of starved, naked corpses piled up ready for burning or burial. The survivors were so thin they looked like living skeletons. When General Eisenhower visited Ohrdurf on April 12 he ordered all American soldiers in the vicinity to tour the camp so that they would know just what they had been fighting against. General Patton was so overcome by the horror of the scene at Ohrdurf that he staggered behind a building to vomit. Jack Hallett, one of the American soldiers who liberated Dachau, recalled:

Remains at Buchenwald 1945 *(Library of Congress)*

The first thing I saw was a stack of bodies that appeared to be about, oh, 20 feet long and about, oh, as high as a man could reach, which looked like cordwood stacked up there, and the thing I'll never forget was the fact that closer inspection found people whose eyes were still blinking maybe three or four deep inside the stack.

At Dachau some GIs assigned to guard captured SS guards were so enraged by what they saw around them that they turned their machine guns on the guards and mowed them down. Other GIs turned captured guards over to prisoners to kill. German civilians from neighboring towns were forced to tour the camps, and sometimes to help bury the dead. Almost always, they denied any knowledge of what had gone on within the walls of the concentration camps.

Even as his empire was collapsing, Hitler still had dreams of ultimate victory. On April 12 the world learned of the death of President Franklin Roosevelt. The strains of war had taken their toll on Roosevelt; in the last six months of his life it was clear to anyone who saw him

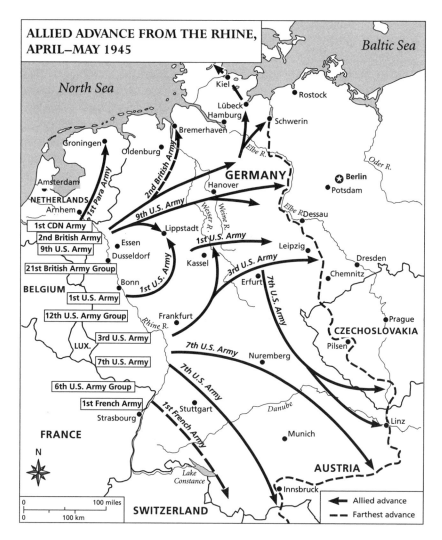

close up that he did not have long to live. Still, his death came as a shock to millions of Americans at home and abroad. Roosevelt had been president for 12 years. It was difficult to imagine life without him, particularly since the new president, Harry Truman, was not well known.

Hitler saw Roosevelt's death as a sign that the tide was about to turn once again in his favor. He ordered that there be no talk of retreat or surrender. Deserters and defeatists would be hung from lampposts in German cities. German armies, whose ranks were increasingly filled with old men and young boys, should fight to the death. Hitler himself intended to stay in his fortified bunker in Berlin and direct the fight against the fast-approaching Red Army.

In these last days of the war there was once again disagreement among Allied leaders on military strategy. Churchill, and some American military commanders, wanted to drive straight on to Berlin, to get there if possible before the Russians. But Eisenhower ordered the Allied armies to turn away from Berlin and to pursue the Germans to the north and the south of the city. A drive on Berlin would cost too many Allied casualties; in any case, the Russians were much closer to the city than the Allies. Eisenhower insisted that the military objective of bringing about the final defeat of the Nazi armies was more important than the political objective of beating the Russians to Berlin.

As the war came to a close, the future relations of the nations that made up the Grand Alliance against Hitler was on many people's minds. On April 25 delegates from around the world began meeting in San Francisco, California, to discuss the creation of a permanent international organization dedicated to keeping the peace. It was to be called the United Nations. On that same day an advance patrol from the U.S. First Army met soldiers from the Soviet army at the town of Torgau on the Elbe River, 75 miles south of Berlin. The eastern and western fronts were now linked together. The Russians threw a party for the Americans, under a red banner proclaiming "Our Greetings to the Brave Troops of the American First Army." Joseph Polowsky, a private in the American patrol, remembered the joyous feeling of Soviet-American friendship that day:

> The Russians had brought some vodka and some German wine and beer. We were real drunk, but not because of the liquor . . . There were accordions and balalaikas and music and dancing. They played Americans songs. Some of the other guys could play the guitar. And there were some from slave-labor camps. Russian girls dancing. It was a strange sight. I was so captivated by the event, that it took possession of me for the rest of my life.

Polowsky survived the war and dedicated his life to working for peace. When he died of cancer in 1983, his last request was to be buried at Torgau in East Germany.

VICTORY OVER NAZISM

As the Allied armies closed in on the last remaining Nazi strongholds, German soldiers and civilians fled westward to surrender to the American and British armies. They were afraid of being captured by the vengeful Soviets. Hitler, finally realizing that the end had come, appointed Admiral Karl Doenitz as his successor. On April 29 Hitler married his longtime companion, Eva Braun; the next day the two of them committed suicide. Their bodies were burned by aides to save them from the fate of Mussolini and his mistress—killed by Italian partisans on April 28 and hung by their heels on a street corner in Milan the following day.

The Third Reich survived its founder's death by one week. The defenders of Berlin surrendered on May 2. On May 5 Field Marshal

Happy second lieutenant William Robertson (left) and Lt. Alexander Sylvashko of the Russian army, shown in front of sign that reads "East Meets West" symbolizing the historic meeting of the Russian and American armies, near Torgau, Germany. *(National Archives)*

Alfred Gustav Jodl, chief of the German General Staff, and several other German officers met with Allied military commanders in the French city of Rheims where Eisenhower had his headquarters. At first the Germans were prepared to talk only about surrendering their armies on the western front. Jodl was stalling, trying to give Germans in the east as much time as possible to make their way out of the Soviet zone of occupation. When the Allies threatened to end the negotiations, the Germans gave in and agreed to surrender on both fronts. On May 7 Jodl signed the surrender documents. The following day, May 8, 1945, the Nazi surrender became official. The news of V-E (Victory in Europe) day was celebrated by cheering crowds in the streets of London, New York, and other Allied cities.

The war in Europe was over. Two members of the Axis Alliance, Germany and Italy, lay defeated. But World War II had not yet come to an end. The war against the last Axis partner, Japan, remained to be won.

22

PACIFIC
ISLAND-HOPPING

Back in 1942, American military strategists had decided on a two-pronged strategy in the Pacific to defeat the Japanese. Gen. Douglas MacArthur's forces would drive the Japanese off New Guinea, then move on to recapture the Philippines. Meanwhile, the forces under the command of Adm. Chester Nimitz in the Central Pacific would "island-hop" their way through the Marshall, Caroline, and Marianas islands; this would put Japan within striking distance of the new American B-29 Superfortress bombers. During the next two years this strategy would prove remarkably successful. The Japanese, masters of the Western Pacific in the spring of 1942, were steadily driven back toward their home islands. These gains did not come cheaply for the Americans. Victory required brutal and bloody fighting against a determined and well-entrenched enemy on some of the most unfavorable terrain in the world.

Americans took their first step on the long journey toward Japan on the island of Guadalcanal in the southern Solomon Islands. Since the spring of 1942 the Japanese had been seizing strongholds in New Guinea and nearby islands, threatening U.S. supply lines to Australia. When Americans learned in early July that the Japanese were building an airbase on Guadalcanal, they quickly geared up for what would be the first U.S. amphibious assault of the war. Some 10,000 U.S. Marines landed on Guadalcanal on August 7, eight months to the day after Pearl Harbor. They met little resistance at first from the Japanese, and quickly seized the island's airstrip. The Americans renamed it Henderson Field after a marine hero of the Battle of Midway.

The marines' early success was no guarantee of final victory. They controlled only a seven-mile-long beachhead on a 90-mile-long island. Japanese reinforcements and supplies were soon pouring down through "the Slot," the sea channel separating the western and eastern Solomons. For months the outcome of the battle remained in doubt. At times the marines wondered whether they would be cut off and abandoned like the Americans at Bataan.

Guadalcanal soon turned into a contest to see which side could keep its forces better supplied and reinforced. With the planes based on Henderson Field, the Americans were able to prevent the Japanese from shipping in reinforcements during the daytime. At night, however, Japanese ships ran what the marines called the "Tokyo Express" through the slot, depositing troops and supplies on Guadalcanal. By November the Japanese actually outnumbered the Americans on the island, although the balance soon swung back the other way.

U.S. Navy task force invades the Marshall Islands, April 1944.
(Library of Congress)

The fighting on the island's nightmarish landscape of steep volcanic slopes, thick decaying jungle, and malaria-ridden swamps was intense. Night after night, waves of Japanese infantry rushed American positions. For three nights in September, Japanese attacks surged against American defenders of Henderson Field in what became known as the Battle of Bloody Ridge. On the night of September 13 alone, the Japanese attacked 12 times shouting "Banzai!" and "Marine, you die!" When the battle ended, there were 1,200 Japanese bodies piled up in front of the Americans. Forty marines had been killed. It was on Guadalcanal that the Japanese soldiers developed their reputation for never surrendering. At the end of the year the U.S. Marines, reinforced by the army, went on the offensive. The Americans gained full control of the island in February 1943. The Guadalcanal campaign's final toll was 24,000 Japanese and 1,752 Americans killed.

Guadalcanal was as much a story of naval warfare as it was of land battles. The day of the American invasion, the Japanese sent a naval task force to attack the American flotilla landing troops on the island. In the ensuing battle of Savo Sound on August 8 and 9 the Japanese scored a major victory, sinking one Australian and three American cruisers, while losing only one of their own cruisers. It was the worst defeat the U.S. Navy had ever suffered at sea. Fortunately the Japanese fleet, fearing counterattack from U.S. carrier-based planes, did not move on to attack the helpless troop transports off Guadalcanal.

Savo Island was the first of seven major naval engagements in the waters around Guadalcanal. So many ships went down in those battles that sailors began to call the area "Ironbottom Sound." In the Battle of the Eastern Solomons in late August, and then in the Battles of Cape d'Esperance and Santa Cruz Islands in October, Americans and Japanese each inflicted losses on the other. The worst American loss was the sinking of the carrier *Hornet* in the Battle of the Santa Cruz Islands. What turned out to be the decisive encounter in mid-November would be called the Battle of Guadalcanal. It began when the U.S. launched a bold nighttime attack on a Japanese task force carrying reinforcements to Guadalcanal. Two Japanese battleships, one cruiser, two destroyers, and seven troop transports were sunk, at a cost of two American cruisers. Two more naval battles were still to be fought—the Battle of Tassafaronga in late November, and the Battle of Rennell Island in late January. By then the Japanese were already convinced that the cost of supplying their troops on Guadalcanal was too heavy. They evacuated their surviving troops from Guadalcanal in February 1943.

Shortly after the marines landed at Guadalcanal, MacArthur's forces on New Guinea also went on the offensive. New Guinea, which lies to the north of Australia, is the second largest island in the world. A steep range of mountains divides the island along its center. In 1942 the Japanese controlled the northern side of the island, while the Allies held the southern side. A Japanese attempt to capture Port Moresby on the southern side was beaten back in the summer and fall of 1942. A mixed force of Americans and Australians then launched their own attack on the northern shore. MacArthur's forces used amphibious landings and, on occasion, paratroop assaults. From 1942 through mid-1944, they leap-frogged their way 1,000 miles westward along New Guinea's northern coast. Along the way they bypassed some Japanese strongholds, leaving them cut off and without hope of resupply.

With New Guinea secured, the Allies had ended the threat to Australia and gained advance airfields which they would need for their eventual return to the Philippines. Meanwhile U.S. Marines and soldiers cleared out the rest of the Solomon Islands, landing on Russell Island in February 1943, on New Georgia in June, on Vella Lavella Island in August, on Choiseul and the Treasury Islands in October, and on Bougainville in November.

The New Guinea campaign included a major U.S. victory at sea, the Battle of the Bismarck Sea. In March 1943 American codebreakers learned that a convoy of troop transports and destroyers was leaving the Japanese base at Rabaul on the island of New Britain for New Guinea. American B-17 heavy bombers and B-25 medium bombers based on Papua in New Guinea intercepted the convoy. They sank all seven transports and five destroyers. Some 3,000 Japanese soldiers drowned. This was the first decisive victory of land-based bombers over a naval fleet.

While MacArthur's troops battled their way across the northern coast of New Guinea, Admiral Nimitz's forces prepared for their first amphibious landings in the central Pacific. On November 20, 1943, Americans landed on Makin and Tarawa in the Gilbert Islands. The Gilberts, 16 small islands located 2,500 miles west of Pearl Harbor, had been occupied by the Japanese in 1941. Makin Island, with 800 Japanese defenders, was taken at relatively light cost in four days fighting by U.S. soldiers. For the Marines on Tarawa—"Bloody Tarawa" as it came to be called—it was a different story.

At least 4,500 Japanese were dug in on Tarawa, the largest of the Gilbert Islands. The Japanese waited in fortified bunkers—"pillboxes" as they were called by the Americans—with heavy concrete walls, covered by roofs of iron rails and coconut logs. A three-hour naval bombardment hardly put a dent in them. American commanders had been warned of tricky tides around the island but took a chance that their landing craft would make it over the coral ledges 500 yards offshore.

Devastation remaining from invasion of Tarawa, November 20, 1943. American dead still float in water near seawall. *(National Archives)*

Seabees

FIGHTING THE WAR WITH BULLDOZERS

IN DECEMBER 1941 THE U.S. NAVY SENT OUT A CALL for volunteers to join its newly established Construction Battalions. Before the war was over, the Construction Battalions had grown to a force of a quarter-million men and played a vital role in supporting the navy and marine amphibious warfare campaign in the Pacific. They were surveyors, carpenters, engineers, and heavy equipment operators, recruited from the ranks of the construction trades, and bringing the tools and skills of their peacetime employment to bear on the battlefront. Like most things military, they were soon referred to by their initials—the "CBs"—which led to the nickname "Seabees."

The Seabee unit insignia depicted a bee in a sailor cap, clenching a submachine gun, a wrench, and a hammer. The men who joined the Seabees were generally several years older than the average combat infantryman in the war, leading to the marine crack, "Never hit a Seabee—he may be your grandfather." A few gray hairs, however, did not keep them from doing their part in the war. The Seabees chose the slogan "Can Do" as their unit motto, and they lived up to it time and again in the island-hopping campaigns of the South Pacific. They often landed, along with their heavy bulldozers and earthmovers, on Japanese-held islands soon after the first waves of marines had hit the beaches, and set about clearing obstacles, and building roads, harbors, and airstrips, sometimes under enemy fire. At war's end, in tribute to the Seabees, Adm. William F. Halsey said that the bulldozer—along with the submarine, radar, and airplane—was one of the four most decisive weapons leading to the American victory in the Pacific.

As it turned out, they should have waited for a higher tide. When the landing craft caught on the reefs, the marines had to wade ashore under heavy fire, suffering hundreds of casualties. Their bodies washed up on shore in the bloody surf.

It took three more days of hard fighting to secure the island. Each pillbox had to be taken by direct assault. It was a grim business. War correspondent Robert Sherrod described one such assault on the first day of fighting:

A Marine jumped over the seawall and began throwing blocks of TNT into a coconut-log pillbox . . . Two more Marines scaled the seawall, one of them carrying a twin-cylindered tank strapped to his shoulders, the other holding the nozzle of the flame-thrower. As another charge of TNT boomed inside the pillbox, causing smoke and dust to billow out, a khaki-clad figure ran out the side entrance. The flame-thrower, waiting for him, caught him in its withering stream of intense fire. As soon as it touched him, the Jap flared up like a piece of celluloid. He was dead instantly but the bullets in his cartridge belt exploded for a full sixty seconds after he had been charred almost to nothingness.

In the end only 17 Japanese survivors crawled out of the wreckage of their defenses to surrender. To capture less than three square miles of an island, 991 marines had to die.

From the Gilbert Islands the Americans moved northwest to the Marshall Islands. Here the lessons of Tarawa were applied. Two months of bombing preceded the invasion to soften up landing sites. Americans landed on Kwajalein atoll on February 1, 1944, killing nearly 8,000 Japanese troops in six days of fighting, at a cost of 372 marines and soldiers. Eniwetok atoll, invaded on February 17, cost more than 2,600 Japanese lives while 339 Americans were killed. Victory in the Marshalls provided air bases allowing U.S. aircraft to control the skies over much of the western Pacific.

After the Marshalls came the Marianas Islands. The largest of the Marianas was Saipan, site of a major Japanese airbase, and defended by 32,000 soldiers. The largest invading force yet assembled in the Pacific, 125,000 marines and soldiers, began landing on Saipan on June 15, 1944. In three weeks of fierce fighting, which cost the lives of almost 3,500 Americans, most of the Japanese garrison was killed in battle. The survivors, along with thousands of Japanese women and children, committed suicide by jumping from high cliffs rather than surrender. Victory on Saipan was followed up by invasions of Guam and Tinian. Guam was the first U.S. possession in the Pacific to be taken back from the Japanese. With the conquest of the Marianas, the U.S. gained bases from which its B-29 Superfortress bombers could reach the Japanese home islands. Saipan was only 1,200 miles from Tokyo, and the new B-29s could deliver their bombs on targets as far as 1,500 miles from their home base.

The U.S. invasion of the Marianas also saw the greatest carrier battle of the war in the Battle of the Philippine Sea on June 19. The

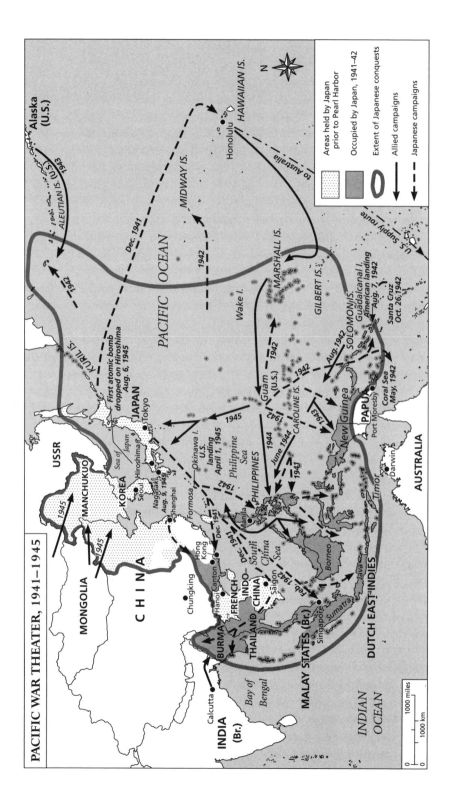

PACIFIC WAR THEATER, 1941–1945

Legend:
- Areas held by Japan prior to Pearl Harbor
- Occupied by Japan, 1941–42
- Extent of Japanese conquests
- Allied campaigns
- Japanese campaigns

Hellcat fighter plane returns to U.S. carrier after striking targets in Tokyo, February 1945. *(National Archives)*

Japanese navy sent nine carriers and other warships to attack the U.S. invasion fleet. The Americans assembled 15 carriers to fight them off. It was an unequal conflict from the start. The U.S. carrier pilots were flying new fighters, F6F Hellcats, which had been specifically designed to outclimb and outdive the Japanese Zero fighters. The Japanese were running out of experienced pilots: those they sent into battle had far less training than the Americans. The result was what American pilots referred to as "the Great Marianas Turkey Shoot": 45 out of 69 Japanese planes in the first wave sent to attack the U.S. carriers were shot down, 98 out of 130 in the second wave, seven out of 47 in the third wave, and 73 out of 82 in the fourth wave. The Americans lost only 30 planes. Three Japanese carriers were sunk, while the U.S. lost only two small ships. After the "turkey shoot" was over, Japanese carrier-based air power was never again a serious factor in the war.

Two years of grueling fighting in the Pacific had welded American fighting forces into an extraordinarily effective military machine. The fighting yet to come, in the Philippines, and on islands like Iwo Jima and Okinawa, would put that machine to its ultimate test.

23

FINAL PUSH IN
THE PACIFIC

American forces in the Pacific spent the final months of 1944 and the spring of 1945 capturing the islands they would need to put them into position for the final assault on Japan. These battles turned out to be among the bloodiest campaigns of the entire war. Although the Americans scored victory after victory, the terrible cost of fighting in the Palaus, the Philippines, Iwo Jima, and Okinawa was a grim preview of what could be expected in the battles on the Japanese mainland.

With the invasion of the Palau Islands, located north of New Guinea and east of the Philippines, the two-pronged American advance in the Pacific was at last joined together. Admiral Nimitz's forces made their contribution to General MacArthur's plans to regain the Philippines by capturing the Palaus, a convenient stepping-stone between New Guinea and the Philippines. The invasion of the main Palau island, Peleliu, was launched on September 15, 1944, by the First Marine Division, under the command of Maj. Gen. William Rupertus. They were later reinforced by soldiers from the Eighty-first Infantry Division. For two full weeks the marines and soldiers fought in temperatures as hot as 115 degrees to conquer the heavily fortified island. The Japanese had learned from earlier battles not to waste men on banzai charges. They fought to the death from their carefully prepared defensive positions. More than 1,000 Americans and 11,000 Japanese were killed in the fighting. Planes based in the Palaus were soon pounding the Philippines in preparation for MacArthur's long-promised return.

FINAL PUSH IN THE PACIFIC

Four U.S. Army divisions landed at 10 A.M., October 20, 1944, on the northeastern coast of Leyte, one of a cluster of mid-size islands lying to the south of the main Philippine island of Luzon. The Americans met only light Japanese resistance. At 1 P.M. General MacArthur, complete with his trademark corncob pipe, boarded a landing craft and headed for shore. It was two and a half years since he had been forced to leave Corregidor. When his landing craft approached the beach, MacArthur stepped out into the knee-deep surf and waded ashore. "People of the Philippines," he declared in a radio broadcast from the invasion beach, "I have returned! By the grace of Almighty God, our forces stand again on Philippine soil." The Americans cleared the island of Japanese defenders by early December, killing 56,263 of the enemy at a cost of 2,888 Americans dead.

The Japanese had hoped to stop the invasion in its first days by means of a complicated naval strategy. The four-day Battle of Leyte Gulf

Japanese forces fought to the death from their heavily fortified positions. *(Library of Congress)*

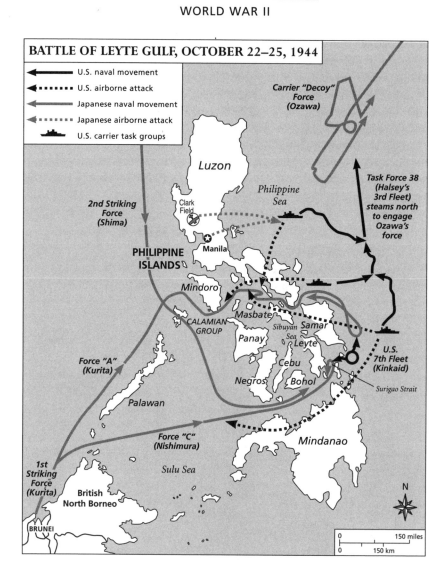

that resulted was the last great naval battle of the Second World War. In terms of the number of ships involved (282) it was one of the greatest naval battles of all time. The American landings in the Leyte Gulf were protected by two large U.S. fleets, the Seventh Fleet under Vice Adm. Thomas C. Kinkaid and the Third Fleet under Adm. William F. Halsey. Japanese naval strategists came up with a plan to lure Halsey's fleet northward away from Leyte with a small decoy fleet including aircraft carriers commanded by Vice Adm. Jisaburo Ozawa. Two other Japanese fleets, with heavy battleships but no carriers, would sail into Leyte Gulf from north and south. They would arrive simultaneously to attack the lightly guarded American troop transports and beaches.

Things started to go wrong with the Japanese plan on October 23. Two U.S. submarines detected the Japanese fleet under Vice Adm. Takeo Kurita, the northern pincer of the Japanese forces closing in on Leyte Gulf. The submarines sank two cruisers and alerted Halsey to the fleet's presence. Halsey's planes attacked the next day, sinking the heavy Japanese battleship *Musashi* in the battle of the Sibuyan Sea. Kurita pulled back the rest of his fleet to temporary safety. He would return to the battle, but the delay meant that the two Japanese pincers would not arrive simultaneously in Leyte Gulf.

Halsey then learned of the presence of the Japanese decoy fleet to the north and set out in pursuit of it. In the battle that followed, his forces sank four Japanese carriers, a cruiser, and two destroyers. It would have been counted a great triumph for Halsey. However, he had left the San Bernardino Strait north of Leyte Gulf unguarded and failed to inform

Gen. Douglas MacArthur (center) wades ashore during initial landings at Leyte, Philippine Islands. *(National Archives)*

U.S. Navy headquarters of his decision to do so. It proved the most controversial decision made by a naval officer during the entire Pacific war.

Meanwhile Admiral Kinkaid's fleet was sailing south to Surigao Strait. He engaged the Japanese fleet commanded by Vice Adm. Ahoji Nishimura, the southern pincer of the Japanese attack on Leyte Gulf. As each Japanese ship sailed through the strait, the guns of the entire Seventh Fleet pounded it in turn, a classic naval maneuver known as "capping the T." Only one Japanese destroyer escaped sinking in the battle, in which Admiral Nishimura was killed. But with Kinkaid doing battle to the south and Halsey pursuing Ozawa's fleet to the north, only a lightly armed force of escort carriers was in Leyte Gulf to protect the invasion. Learning that Halsey had left the northern entrance to the Leyte Gulf unguarded, Kinkaid sent him an urgent message to return. Halsey did, but too late to be of any use in the battle that followed.

Admiral Kurita now brought the remainder of his fleet into Leyte Gulf from the north, attacking the light escort carriers guarding the U.S. troop transports. Planes from the U.S. carriers, which were not armed to do battle with heavy warships, nevertheless managed to sink three of Kurita's cruisers. The battle still could have turned into a disaster for the Americans had Kurita continued his attack. But he suddenly lost his nerve and withdrew his fleet from Leyte Gulf before it could do real damage to the U.S. invasion forces. The Japanese had almost pulled off their plan, but luck that day was with the Americans. With total Japanese losses of four carriers, three battleships, and six cruisers, the Battle of Leyte Gulf marked the end of the Japanese Imperial Navy as an effective fighting force.

It was during the Battle of Leyte Gulf that the Japanese first employed a new and menacing weapon against the Americans. This was the use of kamikaze (Japanese, "divine wind") suicide attacks by Japanese airmen. The kamikaze pilots tried to crash their planes, which were packed with high explosives, into American ships. The land-based kamikazes would be used in great numbers off Iwo Jima and Okinawa. By the end of the war they had sunk 30 and damaged more than 300 American ships.

With the conquest of Leyte completed, the Americans turned their attention to the main Philippine island, Luzon. They landed on Luzon on January 9, 1945, and over the next few months fought 250,000 Japanese defenders in the largest land battles of the Pacific the-

A Japanese kamikaze (upper left) moments before crashing into the side of the battleship *Missouri,* 1945 *(National Archives)*

ater. By February 3 the Americans had fought their way to the outskirts of Manila. It took a month of house-to-house fighting to clear the Japanese out of the city, a battle in which 100,000 Filipino civilians were caught in the crossfire and killed. Corregidor, site of the Americans' last stand in the Philippines three years earlier, was recaptured February 26.

Even before the fighting in Luzon ended, the Americans were pressing on with their offensive, seeking to gain a base of attack close to

Japan. For a long time, U.S. strategists dreamed of launching a major assault on Japanese forces in China; the plan was to eventually use the country as the base for the invasion of the Japanese home islands. But the Chinese government was weak and corrupt, more interested in laying away arms for a postwar battle with the Chinese Communists than in fighting the Japanese occupiers. The American commander in what was called the China-Burma-India (CBI) theater was Maj. Gen. Joseph "Vinegar Joe" Stilwell, one of the most capable U.S. generals. Chinese and American troops under Stilwell's command played an important role in the Allied offensive to drive the Japanese out of Burma. But Stilwell's talents were wasted in a futile attempt to get China's leader, Generalissimo Chiang Kai-shek, to improve China's fighting capabilities. Since China was not available as a base for invading Japan, the Americans would have to look elsewhere.

One of the places they considered was Iwo Jima, eight square miles of volcanic rubble, less than 800 miles from the main Japanese island. Iwo Jima was used by the Japanese as a fighter airbase. The Americans wanted it for the same purpose and also to serve as a place where B-29s crippled over Japan could make emergency landings. Two U.S. Marine Divisions of the V Amphibious Corps under Maj. Gen. Harry

The U.S. carrier *Franklin,* 60 miles off the Japanese coast, listing from an attack by a Japanese dive bomber *(Library of Congress)*

Schmidt landed on Iwo Jima on February 19, 1945. There they confronted 20,000 Japanese dug into an extensive system of caves, tunnels, and pillboxes.

The conquest of Iwo Jima proved the hardest fight the marines faced in the Pacific. From the moment they went ashore they were under continuous heavy bombardment from well-hidden gun positions. The marines, crowded on the beaches, found no shelter from the shelling. The medical stations, filled with wounded men, were repeatedly hit. Journalist Robert Sherrod wrote of the bodies scattered on the beach on the second day of the invasion: "They died with the greatest possible violence. Nowhere in the Pacific have I seen such badly mangled bodies. Many were cut squarely in half. Legs and arms lay 50 feet away from any body."

The slopes of Mount Suribachi, an extinct volcano that towered above the invasion beach, were slowly cleared of Japanese emplacements by marines wielding flamethrowers. American spirits were lifted on February 23 when a marine patrol made it to the top of Suribachi and raised the American flag. A photograph by Associated Press photographer Joe Rosenthal of the raising of a second and larger flag shortly afterward became the model for the U.S. Marine Corps monument in Arlington Cemetery in Washington, D.C. Even with control of Suribachi, many days of hard fighting still remained on Iwo Jima. The battle cost 6,821 American lives in more than a month's fighting. Twenty-seven Medals of Honor were awarded to the men who took the island. Admiral Nimitz later wrote, "Among the Americans who served on Iwo Island uncommon valor was a common virtue."

From Iwo Jima the next step toward Japan was Okinawa. The 67-mile-long island was considered part of Japan, although located 350 miles south of the main Japanese islands. At least 120,000 Japanese soldiers defended the island. The U.S. invasion in April 1945 was the greatest amphibious operation of the Pacific War, with 1,300 ships assembled offshore. The battle, involving 300,000 marines and soldiers, was to last 82 days. Two army and two marine divisions under the command of Lt. Gen. Simon Bolivar Buckner went ashore without difficulty on April 1. They met heavy resistance as they moved inland. The worst kamikaze attacks of the war hit the American fleet stationed offshore; nearly 350 kamikazes tried to hit American ships on April 6 and 7 alone. The Japanese also sent in their remaining large battleship, the

Marines raise the flag on Mount Suribachi, in the Battle of Iwo Jima.
(Library of Congress)

Yamato, on a suicide mission of its own. With enough fuel for only a
one-way trip, the *Yamato* sailed to attack the American fleet. It was sunk
on April 7 before it even had a chance to fire its guns.

Some 12,000 Americans, including General Buckner, were killed in
combat in the invasion. However, 110,000 Japanese soldiers died,

including Lt. Gen. Mitsuru Ushijima, commander of the defending forces. As the Americans closed in on his headquarters, Ushijima put on his full-dress uniform and committed hara-kiri (ritual suicide) by plunging a knife into his own stomach. After this, one of his aides cut off his head with a samurai sword.

The fighting in the Pacific was fierce. E. B. Sledge, a veteran of the First Marine Division, who fought on Peleliu and Okinawa, later reflected on the difference between the European and Pacific theaters in the Second World War. On occasions he saw his buddies kill wounded Japanese soldiers rather than take them as prisoners. Some Americans would knock out gold teeth from the mouths of Japanese corpses. The Japanese willingness to fight to the death seemed to make them something other than human to the Americans who fought them:

> The war I knew was totally savage . . . Our attitude towards the Japanese was different than the one we had toward the Germans. My brother who was with the Second Infantry Division in the Battle of the Bulge, wounded three times, said when things were hopeless for the Germans, they surrendered . . . When they surrendered, they were guys just like us. With the Japanese, it was not that way. At Peleliu, my company took two prisoners. At Okinawa, we took about five. We had orders not to kill the wounded, to try to take prisoners. If they surrendered, they'd give you information. But the feeling was [too] strong . . .

The nature of the fighting on Iwo Jima and Okinawa raised fears about the coming invasion of Japan, which was scheduled for November 1945. If things went as planned, some 750,000 men were scheduled to join in the invasion of Kyushu, the southernmost of the four Japanese home islands. American casualties were projected at as many as 268,000 killed and wounded, many more than the total lost to that point in the Pacific fighting. That would still leave the largest and most important Japanese island, Honshu, to be invaded the following spring. All over the Pacific—and in Europe and the United States—American servicemen in the summer of 1945 were wondering: Would they survive the years of hard fighting that were still expected?

24
ATOMIC WARFARE

Three years of ground and naval battles in the Pacific finally put the United States in a position in late 1944 where it could launch a strategic bombing campaign against Japan. This time bombing did all that the air force generals said it would. Japan surrendered without a single American infantryman having to die on its beaches. Tens of thousands of bombs were dropped on Japan, but it was two bombs dropped on Hiroshima and Nagasaki that really made the difference. The development and use of the atomic bomb not only brought World War II to an end. It also guaranteed that the world would be a very different place after 1945 than it had been before 1939.

The Japanese military had waged war without regard for civilian life. In China millions of civilians died at the hands of Japanese aggressors between 1931 and 1945. In war, unfortunately, the crimes of the guilty are often paid for by the innocent. Japan's civilian government and population had little control over the actions of the Japanese military. Civilian politicians who attempted to restrict the army's aggressiveness in China in the 1930s were assassinated by military killers. The war unleashed in the Pacific by Japan's military men would in time come home and cause terrible hardship and loss for Japan's civilians.

Japan's cities made good targets for bombers. Fires spread easily in the country's wood and paper cities; a fire set off by a natural disaster, the earthquake of 1923, destroyed half of Tokyo and killed 100,000 people. For much of the war Japan was out of range of American bombers. The carrier-launched Doolittle raid of April 1942 had been a valuable

U.S. ARMY AIR FORCES STRATEGIC AIR OFFENSIVE AGAINST JAPANESE-HELD TERRITORY, 1944–1945

Approximate area of Japanese Empire and occupied territories at the start of the strategic air offensive, June 1944

● Bombing targets

Normal maximum radius of action 2,575 km (1,600 miles)

morale booster for Americans. It had done little damage to Tokyo. Since all of Doolittle's planes were lost when they crash-landed in China, it was not a tactic that could be repeated very often.

With the development of the new, long-range B-29 Superfortress bomber, the bombing of Japan became a practical matter for the first time. B-29s based in China began hitting targets in Japan in June 1943. Because of the great distance involved, and the difficulty in getting fuel to the Chinese bases, these raids were still few and far between. The capture of the Mariana Islands in 1944, just 1,300 miles from Tokyo, at last gave the United States the bases it needed for a full-scale bombing campaign. B-29 raids by the new Twenty-first Bomber Command based in the Marianas were launched in November 1944.

At first the air force tried daylight "precision" attacks against Japanese factories, but winter clouds reduced their effectiveness. In January 1945 the Twenty-first Bomber Command got a new commander, Maj. Gen. Curtis LeMay, who had commanded the Eighth Air Force in England before being transferred to the Pacific. In February, LeMay ordered a change in tactics. From then on American bombers would make nighttime raids, dropping incendiary (fire-starting) bombs on Japan's cities. After several trial runs, LeMay launched an all-out assault on Tokyo.

On the evening of March 9, 334 B-29s pounded Tokyo with incendiary bombs. High winds fanned the flames, creating a firestorm in which the heat from the fires produced even higher winds, which spread the fire everywhere. Tokyo's citizens burned to death or suffocated when the oxygen was burned from the air around them. Some took refuge in the Sumida River, only to die when the fires along the shore raised the temperature of the water to the boiling point. Between 80,000 and 100,000 people lost their lives that night; 250,000 homes were destroyed. Osaka and other major cities received similar treatment in the months that followed. By July nearly 500,000 civilians had died in the bombings.

Japan's military defeats in the Pacific and the suffering of its civilians began to affect the thinking of some of the country's leaders. Emperor Hirohito and some civilian leaders were now opposed to continuing the war to the bitter end. They had to act quietly because they feared that any open move for peace would spark a military takeover. At a conference on June 22, 1945, Hirohito asked government and military leaders to consider ways to end the war. In the summer of 1945 Japanese diplomats contacted the Soviet government. They hoped to get Russia to act as the middleman with the United States in peace negotiations.

Of great concern to peace-minded Japanese leaders was the Allied demand for Japan's "unconditional surrender." At the very least, the Japanese wanted to preserve the rule of the emperor if they had to surrender. Unknown to the Japanese, U.S. experts had already recommended to the president that, after Japan's surrender, the country should be allowed to keep its emperor, so long as his powers were strictly limited. The United States knew of the Japanese "peace feelers." But most American political and military leaders doubted the sincerity of the Japanese desire for peace. Publicly the Japanese government continued to call on its citizens to be prepared to fight to the death in the case of an American invasion. Japan's leaders had begun their turn toward peace too late. By the summer of 1945 the Americans had developed a new weapon, the atomic bomb. They were convinced this would swiftly bring the Japanese to their knees.

ATOMIC WARFARE

When Alexander Sachs brought Albert Einstein's letter about nuclear fission to President Roosevelt in October 1939, Roosevelt had responded, "This requires action." Action was at first slow in coming. When a government-appointed "Uranium Committee" began holding meetings in the spring of 1940 to discuss the possibilities for developing an atomic weapon, neither Leo Szilard nor Enrico Fermi were asked to participate. Even though the refugee physicists had been the first to draw the government's attention to nuclear fission, they were kept off the committee because they were not American citizens. As the decision was explained to Alexander Sachs, "these matters are secret." Acting on his own, Szilard kept sending information to Roosevelt through Sachs about the state of current research in nuclear fission. He also reported on the rumors that the Nazis were moving ahead at full speed with their own research.

In England, as in the United States, refugee physicists played an important role in spurring research on nuclear fission. By the spring of 1940 they had worked out a rough idea of how an atomic bomb could be built. The British government became interested and in the spring of 1941 sent a secret report to its American ally. The British suggested that it might be possible to build a bomb within as short as two years' time. Seeing this report, the attitude of the U.S. government changed dramatically. The atomic bomb was no longer just a distant theoretical possibility. It was a practical weapon that might win the war for the Allies—or lose it if the Germans developed it first.

In late 1941 the U.S. government launched a vastly expanded program of atomic research, code-named the "Manhattan Project." The United States and Britain agreed to share all their research on the bomb, which would be built in the United States. Thousands of the nation's top scientists were recruited to work on the project, including the refugee physicists. Fermi and Szilard worked in a laboratory at the University of Chicago where important experiments with chain reactions were performed. A nonscientist, Brig. Gen. Leslie R. Groves, was given overall command of the Manhattan Project. The nuclear physicist J. Robert Oppenheimer was made director of the giant new laboratory in Los Alamos, New Mexico, where much of the most crucial research was done. Oppenheimer, probably more than any other man, deserves the title of "father of the atomic bomb."

Philip Morrison, a physicist who worked at Los Alamos under Oppenheimer, described the laboratory as an "army post with physicists":

Soviet Espionage and the Manhattan Project

NO WARTIME SECRET WAS MORE CLOSELY GUARDED in the United States than the existence of the vast enterprise devoted to developing and building an atomic bomb. An army of physicists, engineers, machinists, and others worked in secret laboratories and workshops, under armed guard, in such locations as Oak Ridge, Tennessee, and Los Alamos, New Mexico. But tight security proved to no avail. America's wartime enemies, Germany and Japan, were kept in ignorance of the atomic bomb project. But spies working on behalf of America's wartime ally, the Soviet Union, penetrated the ring of security.

At Los Alamos, Klaus Fuchs, a German refugee physicist, along with Ted Hall, an American physics student, and David Greenglass, an army machinist, provided Soviet spies with details on the design of the atomic bomb. All three were dedicated communists, sympathetic to the Soviet cause, and worried about the postwar consequences of a U.S. monopoly on nuclear weapons. Soviet physicists would eventually have been able to develop the bomb on their own, but information provided by Fuchs, Hall, and Greenglass cut a year or more off the time it would have taken them. The Soviet Union exploded its first nuclear device in 1949. Fuchs and Greenglass were both arrested for espionage, confessed their crime, and served long prison sentences. Hall fell under suspicion but was never arrested. The harshest penalty fell upon Julius and Ethel Rosenberg, Greenglass's brother-in-law and sister. They had recruited Greenglass as a spy and passed along the information he provided to Soviet agents. Maintaining their innocence to the end, the Rosenbergs went to the electric chair in New York's Sing Sing Prison in 1953, the only Americans to be executed for the crime of espionage in the 20th century.

When I walked down the street, I knew everyone personally. We never had such a sense of fraternity in a little community before. Of course, it was secret. It was surrounded by guards. We could not go out without permission. Our mail was censored, our telephone calls were interrupted. We consented to all this. The payment . . . for our acceptance of control and isolation was that we be allowed to talk freely, one with the

Mushroom cloud rises over Nagasaki after second atomic bomb is dropped, August 8, 1945. *(National Archives)*

other. You knew all that was going on. Within the community there was complete openness . . . There were no secrets to which we were not privy. We were inventing the secrets.

In the spring of 1945 as the bomb neared completion, Leo Szilard was once again a worried man. Since December 1944 the Manhattan Project physicists had known that the Nazis were not far enough along in their research to build an atomic bomb before the war ended. With that threat gone, Szilard and some other physicists began to think about the effect that the use of the bomb might have on international relations. Szilard tried to set up a meeting with Roosevelt in the spring of 1945. He wrote a memo to the president in which he warned that the use of the atomic bomb on Japan might lead to a "race in the production of these devices between the United States and Russia." Roosevelt died before Szilard got to meet with him.

In any case, the pressures to use the bomb were now too great to be resisted. At 5:30 A.M. on July 16, 1945, the first atomic bomb was exploded at a desert test site near the Alamogordo Air Base in New Mexico. The explosion created a shock wave that broke a window 125 miles away, and a light so bright that a blind woman insisted she had seen it. To cover up the nature of the test, the government put out the story that an ammunition dump on the base had exploded.

Out in the Pacific the specially trained 509th Composite Group of the U.S. Army Air Force, based on the island of Tinian, began making practice runs over Japan in late July. On August 6, 1945, a B-29 bomber nicknamed *Enola Gay*, flown by Col. Paul Tibbets, approached the Japanese city of Hiroshima. The *Enola Gay* was accompanied by two other bombers carrying cameras and scientific instruments. At 8:15 A.M. the B-29 dropped the one bomb in its load. It exploded 45 seconds later at an altitude of 2,000 feet above the city. In a single instant four square miles of the city around ground zero (the spot where the bomb would have hit if it had fallen to the ground) vanished. Almost nothing was left standing and 100,000 people were killed. As the plane flew away from its target a large mushroom-shaped cloud of dust, debris, and fire churned up over the city. Tens of thousands more people who escaped immediate injury would die in the years

Ruins of Hiroshima—epicenter of atomic bomb drop—October 1945
(National Archives)

The USS Indianapolis

THE USS *INDIANAPOLIS,* A HEAVY CRUISER WITH A crew of nearly 1,200 men, would have the unhappy distinction of being the last major U.S. warship sunk by hostile action in World War II.

The *Indianapolis* was launched in 1931 and was among the few battleships in the Pacific Fleet that was not at Pearl Harbor on December 7, 1941. The ship and its crew racked up a distinguished combat record in the fighting that followed. The *Indianapolis's* eight-inch guns provided support for marine landings in the Marshall, Gilbert, and Mariana Islands. The ship took part in the battle of the Philippine Sea in June 1944 and was on hand for the invasion of Iwo Jima. At Okinawa, the *Indianapolis* served as the fleet flagship, until it was damaged by kamikaze attack in March 1945.

The *Indianapolis* returned to California for repairs, but in mid-July 1945 was given another important assignment. It delivered an atomic bomb to the B-29 base on Tinian Island, the bomb that would be dropped on the Japanese city of Hiroshima a few weeks later.

The *Indianapolis* then set sail for Okinawa. But on July 30 the ship was struck by torpedoes launched by a Japanese submarine. It capsized and sunk within two minutes, too quickly for an SOS signal to be sent. Except for its crew, clinging to debris or floating in their life preservers, no one knew that the ship had gone down. So for three days and nights, without food or water, facing constant shark attack, the men of the *Indianapolis* waited for rescue. Finally, completely by chance, a passing naval patrol plane spotted them. By the time rescuers showed up, only 318 of the crew's original 1,199 remained alive.

ahead of the effects of exposure to the radiation released by the bomb's explosion. Three days later a second bomb was dropped, on the city of Nagasaki, killing 40,000.

For the marines and GIs who would have had to storm the beaches in the upcoming invasion of Japan, the feeling on hearing the news from Hiroshima and Nagasaki was one of happiness. Paul Fussell, a 21-year-old second lieutenant in 1945 who had already been badly wounded once in the war, later remembered, "We cried with relief and joy. We were going to live. We were going to grow up to adulthood after all." For the physicists who built the bomb, the news brought mixed feelings. Philip Morrison was on Tinian in August 1945, along with other physicists from the Manhattan Project, to supervise the loading of the bombs on the planes that would carry them to Japan:

> We heard the news of Hiroshima from the airplane itself, a coded message. When they returned, we didn't see them. The generals had them. But then the people came back with photographs. I remember looking at them with awe and terror. We knew a terrible thing had been unleashed. The men had a great party that night to celebrate, but we didn't go. Almost no physicists went to it. We obviously killed a hundred thousand people and that was nothing to have a party about. The reality confronts you with things you could never anticipate.

Japan could no longer put off the inevitable. On August 10 the Japanese government agreed to surrender, asking only that the emperor

Signing of Japanese surrender on USS *Missouri*—September 2, 1945
(Library of Congress)

ATOMIC WARFARE

continue to rule. The United States replied that the emperor would be subject to the orders of the Supreme Commander of the Allied Powers during the postwar occupation of Japan. The emperor accepted this condition on August 14, which was celebrated in the United States as V-J (Victory over Japan) Day. On August 15 Hirohito's voice was heard on the Japanese radio, telling his people that Japan had lost the war.

On September 2, 1945, the Japanese signed the surrender documents aboard the U.S. battleship *Missouri* anchored in Tokyo Bay. Gen. Douglas MacArthur accepted the Japanese surrender on behalf of the Allies, declaring:

> It is my earnest hope and indeed the hope of all mankind that from this solemn occasion a better world shall emerge out of the blood and carnage of the past—a world founded upon faith and understanding—a world dedicated to the dignity of man and the fulfillment of his most cherished wish—for freedom, tolerance and justice.

World War II was over.

25

RENDEZVOUS
WITH DESTINY

———◆{ɷɷ————————————————————————

The Second World War was over, and around the world people began to rebuild shattered lives and shattered countries. It had been the most destructive war in history. The loss in human life was immense. No one knows how many people died in the war, though estimates run to 40 million and more. The Soviet Union alone lost 27 million dead, civilian and military. Poland lost the highest proportion of its population, with 300,000 soldiers and 5.8 million civilians (2 million of them Polish Jews) killed—15 percent of Poland's prewar population. The figures for China are particularly unreliable, but the total number of military and civilian dead may have been as many as 13.5 million. Hitler's war cost Germany the lives of more than 4 million of its soldiers and civilians. Japan lost 2 million dead, Yugoslavia lost 1.5 million, France lost 600,000, Britain lost 400,000 and Italy lost 300,000. The United States got off relatively lightly: American military casualties totaled 290,000 killed, 670,000 wounded. About 6,000 American civilians, most of them sailors in the merchant marine, lost their lives.

The effects of the war would be felt for decades. Across Europe peace soon turned into a "cold war" between the Soviet Union and its former Western allies. By 1946 Winston Churchill declared that an "iron curtain" had descended across the eastern half of Europe. Poland, Hungary, Romania, Bulgaria, Yugoslavia, Albania, Czechoslovakia, and East Germany were ruled by communist governments aligned with the Soviet Union. In the wartime summit meetings at Tehran, Iran, in 1943

The "Big Three" of the New Order—Clement Attlee (left), Harry Truman (center), and Joseph Stalin (right)—at the Potsdam Conference in Germany, August 1, 1945. *(Library of Congress)*

and at Yalta in the Soviet Union in 1945, the Big Three—Roosevelt, Churchill, and Stalin—had discussed the postwar settlement. Roosevelt had hoped to see the principles of the Atlantic Charter, especially that of self-determination, used as the basis for the settlement. He also told Stalin that he understood the Soviet desire to have friendly governments along its western border. In the end, Stalin got his friendly governments, but the peoples of eastern Europe did not get self-determination. Yugoslavia was an exception: Its Communist government was put in power by Tito's partisans, not by the Red Army, and in 1948 Yugoslavia broke with the Soviet Union to pursue an independent foreign policy.

Before the war the actions and opinions of a number of great powers or would-be great powers—England, France, Germany, Italy, Japan, the United States, and the Soviet Union—weighed heavily in international relations. For several decades after the war the actions and opinions of only two superpowers—the United States and the Soviet Union—dominated international relations. The Free World, centered on the United States, confronted the Soviet bloc, which centered around the Soviet Union. After 1949 China became part of the Soviet bloc although, as in Yugoslavia, the Chinese Communists came to power on their own and later broke with the Soviet Union.

In this divided new world, there could be no postwar retreat to isolationism by the United States. Although it greatly reduced the size of its armed forces from their Second World War peak, the United States maintained a high level of military preparedness in the decades after the war. For the first time American troops were stationed in bases around the world. In 1947 President Harry Truman pledged in his "Truman doctrine" that the United States would come to the aid of any nation threatened by communist attack or takeover. That same year the United States extended economic aid through the Marshall Plan to the nations of western Europe to rebuild their war-torn economies. Although America was now the most powerful nation in the world, in some ways Americans felt more at risk than they ever had before. This was particularly true after the Soviet Union successfully tested its first atomic bomb in 1949. The arms race that Leo Szilard warned against in 1945 drained the economies of both sides in the cold war.

The old European colonial empires were fatally weakened by the war. The principles of the Atlantic Charter were taken to heart in ways that at least one of its authors, Winston Churchill, would not have approved of. A wave of nationalism swept across Africa and Asia, leading to demands for self-determination and independence. The nation of Israel was created in what had been British-ruled Palestine in 1948. That same year Pakistan and India gained their independence from the British Empire. The Dutch East Indies became the independent nation of Indonesia in 1949. After a bitter war, French Indochina was carved up into the independent nations of Laos, Cambodia, and Vietnam, itself separated into North Vietnam and South Vietnam. In 1951 the former Italian colony of Libya gained its independence, and between 1956 and the mid-1960s the French, British, and Belgian colonies in Africa became independent nations.

The peace that followed World War II fell far short of the idealistic principles expressed in the Atlantic Charter and Roosevelt's Four Freedoms speech. But at least there was peace. Only a quarter-century had divided the start of World War I in 1914 from the start of World War II in 1939. In the 60-odd years since the start of the Second World War the major powers have avoided any direct military clashes. The principles of collective security, democracy, and self-determination survived the war, even if they were not universally applied. The United Nations was able in at least some instances to settle international disputes without violence. The defeated Axis powers—Japan, Italy, and the western half of Germany—were transformed after the war into democracies. And in 1989–90, 45 years after the end of the Second World War, the nations of eastern Europe finally secured the right to self-determination promised them in the Atlantic Charter.

The General Assembly Hall of the United Nations, in New York City
(UN Photo 169,894)

In one of his most famous speeches, delivered five years before Pearl Harbor, President Roosevelt declared:

> There is a mysterious cycle in human events. To some generations much is given. Of other generations much is expected. This generation of Americans has a rendezvous with destiny.

The generation of Americans who lived through and fought in the Second World War did indeed have a "rendezvous with destiny." They saw their nation and the world transformed in the global struggle in which they played so large a role.

Glossary

aircraft carrier   A warship equipped with a deck for the taking off and landing of aircraft and storage space for the aircraft.

ammunition   The materials used in discharging firearms or any weapon that throws projectiles, including powder, shot, shrapnel, bullets, cartridges, and the means of igniting and exploding them, such as primers and fuses. Chemicals, bombs, grenades, and mines are also ammunition.

amphibious warfare   The landing of troops and equipment from the sea in boats or vehicles that can move into shallow water; the vehicles are able to travel up onto the beach.

anti-Semitism   Hostility to Jews as a people and a religion; a key tenet of Nazi ideology.

appeasement   The act of acceding to the belligerent demands of a group or country, usually involving a sacrifice of principle or justice.

armada   A large fleet of warships.

armistice   A truce or agreement by warring parties to cease hostilities, at least temporarily but usually with the intention of negotiating a permanent peace. The best known armistice of modern times is the one signed by the Allies and Central Powers that brought World War I to an end at 11 A.M. on November 11, 1918.

arsenal   A workshop where arms and ammunition are manufactured; a warehouse where arms and other military materials are stored.

Aryan   Originally a prehistoric people who spoke Indo-European; in Nazi ideology, a "racially pure" German.

attrition   The wearing down of enemy resources and ability to continue armed conflict, as when military attacks are launched not primarily to take ground but to kill as many of the opponent's troops as possible.

bazooka   A cylindrical rocket launcher carried by infantry in World War II. It fired a projectile intended to penetrate the armor plating of a tank or other military vehicle.

beachhead   The area that is the first objective of a military force landing on an enemy shore.

blackout   The extinguishing of all visible lights in a city as a measure of protection against enemy attack.

bridgehead   A position held on the enemy side of a river to permit and defend the crossing of friendly troops.

casualties   In the case of battles, total casualties usually include those killed, wounded, taken prisoner, and missing in action. When reported for an entire war, casualties may also include those who die in noncombat activities and from diseases contracted while in theaters of war.

civil war   A war between parties, regions, or ethnic groups within a single country.

coalition   A combination or alliance arranged on a temporary basis, as among wartime allies.

collective security   A policy or principle in international affairs, according to which many countries band together to guarantee the security of individual countries against foreign aggression.

communism   The theory and system of social organization that is based on common or state ownership of industry, agriculture, and all other economic enterprises; a system of government based on the dictatorship of the Communist Party.

convoy   A formation of ships in which the most important vessels—often cargo or troop carriers—are surrounded by smaller, faster-moving combat ships to protect them from enemy attack.

C rations   Nutritionally balanced rations developed for the U.S. Army troops in the field during World War II, they came in 12-ounce cans and included a main course of meat and vegetables plus hard biscuits. When possible, the troops would heat the meat dish in the can. The *C* is sometimes said to be derived from *combat,* sometimes from *canned.* (See also K rations.)

cruiser   Medium-tonnage warship designed for high speed and long cruising distance.

cryptography The process or art of writing in secret characters or in cipher (code).

depth charge An explosive device dropped from a ship or airplane into water, set to explode when it reaches a certain depth, used to combat submarines.

dive-bomber A combat aircraft that drops its bomb load while diving toward its target.

draft A form of involuntary military recruitment through the selection of individuals from the civilian population to join a nation's armed forces. Also known as *conscription.*

embargo An order from a government prohibiting the movement of merchant ships from or into its own ports. It may also be issued by a government to prohibit trade, whether specific or all kinds, with foreign nations.

espionage The systematic use of spies by a government to learn the military and political secrets of another nation.

fascism A form of single-party dictatorship, fostering an ideology of extreme nationalism, military aggression, anticommunism, and (often) racism.

glider A motorless, heavier-than-air craft, towed into high altitude position by a motor-driven aircraft, and then cut loose to deliver troops and supplies to the battlefront.

hedgerow A form of agricultural fencing common in western Europe (especially the Normandy region of France), in which a row of bushes or trees planted on an earthen embankment forms a hedge barrier.

isolationism A policy of nonparticipation in international affairs.

K rations Nutritionally balanced rations plus other items (such as cigarettes, matches, candy, gum) that came in stiff packets that were lighter to carry than the C ration cans. The *K* is sometimes said to be derived from *kit,* sometimes from a man by the name of Keys said to have developed this kit. (See also C rations.)

latrine Communal toilet facilities, especially in a military camp or barracks.

logistics The branch of military science concerned with the transportation and supply of troops in the field.

machine gun   A small arm able to deliver a rapid and continuous fire of bullets, until the weapon's magazine or firing belt is depleted.

merchant marine   The crews and vessels of a nation that are involved in commerce.

meteorologist   A scientist who studies weather patterns and uses this knowledge to predict future weather conditions.

mine   A device containing an explosive charge, placed in a camouflaged setting, and designed to explode and kill enemy soldiers or destroy enemy vehicles when they are in its immediate vicinity.

morphine   A narcotic derived from opium, which when inserted into the bloodstream can dull pain or induce unconsciousness.

Nazism   The movement founded by Adolf Hitler that exalted German national and racial superiority, preached anti-Semitism and anticommunism, and called for the elimination of democratic government.

neutrality   The status of a nation that does not participate in a war between other nations.

nuclear fission   The breakdown of the atomic nucleus of an element into two or more nuclei, with the conversion of part of the original mass into energy.

pacifist   An opponent of all wars on the principle of opposition to killing.

partisan   A member of a group of irregular troops engaged in guerrilla warfare.

propaganda   News and commentary on news released by a government in wartime, intended to persuade domestic and foreign audiences of the righteousness of the government's cause in the war.

quartermaster   Military officer charged with providing shelter, clothing, provisions, fuel, and other materials to troops in the field.

radar   A device used to determine the presence and location of an object, such as a plane or ship, by measuring the time it takes for the echo of a radio signal to return after bouncing off it.

rear echelon   That part of a military force in the field that does not serve in combat in the front lines, but rather provides command structure, services, and material to the soldiers at the front.

reconnaissance A search made for useful military information in the field by means of observation of enemy positions and movements and the physical landscape upon which battles are likely to occur.

refugee One who flees to safety, especially to a foreign country, in a time of political upheaval or warfare.

reparations Enforced compensation in the form of cash, labor, or materials on the part of a defeated nation to other nations or people it is accused of having unjustly harmed in wartime

sabotage Damage done to the effective working of industrial production, communication, or transportation by agents working behind enemy lines.

semiautomatic A self-loading rifle or other firearm, such as the American M-1 Garand rifle in World War II.

shell shock A nervous condition or mental disorder experienced by frontline soldiers due to the cumulative strain of modern warfare.

sonar A device used to determine the presence and location of objects under the surface of the water, such as enemy submarines, by measuring the direction and return time of a sound echo. The word is an acronym formed from *so*und, *na*vigation, and *r*anging.

sortie From takeoff to landing, the flight of an individual aircraft on a combat mission.

supply dump A place where a large quantity of military materials, including ammunition, fuel, or food, has been gathered prior to distribution to soldiers in the field.

torpedo A self-propelled, cigar-shaped explosive device, launched from a submarine, torpedo boat, or airplane, and designed to sink an enemy ship.

totalitarian A system of government in which no political opposition is permitted, and the state claims the authority to regulate virtually all aspects of public and private life.

Further Reading

NONFICTION

Abzug, Robert H. *Inside the Vicious Heart: Americans and the Liberation of Nazi Concentration Camps.* New York: Oxford, 1985.

Ambrose, Stephen E. *Band of Brothers: E Company, 506th Regiment, 101st Airborne, From Normandy to Hitler's Eagle's Nest.* New York: Simon and Schuster, 1992.

———. *Citizen Soldiers: The U.S. Army from the Normandy Beaches to the Bulge to the Surrender of Germany.* New York: Simon and Schuster, 1997.

———. *D-Day, June 6, 1944: The Climactic Battle of World War II.* New York: Simon and Schuster, 1994.

———. *The Victors: Eisenhower and His Boys: The Men of World War II.* New York: Simon and Schuster, 1998.

Blum, John Morton. *V Was for Victory: Politics and American Culture During World War II.* New York: HBJ, 1976.

Boyer, Paul. *By the Bomb's Early Light: American Thought and Culture at the Dawn of the Atomic Age.* Chapel Hill: University of North Carolina Press, 1994.

Bradley, John H., and Jack W. Dice. *The Second World War: Asia and the Pacific.* Wayne, N.J.: Avery, 1984.

Brokaw, Tom. *The Greatest Generation.* New York: Dell, 2001.

Buchanan, Albert Russell. *The United States and World War II.* 2 Vols. New York: Harper and Row, 1964.

Crane, Conrad. *Bombs, Cities, and Civilians: American Airpower Strategy in World War II.* Lawrence: University Press of Kansas, 1993.

Crosby, Harry H. *A Wing and a Prayer: The "Bloody 100th" Bomb Group of the U.S. Eighth Air Force in Action over Europe in World War II.* New York: HarperCollins, 1993.

Cutler, Thomas J. *The Battle of Leyte Gulf.* New York: HarperCollins, 1994.

D'Este, Carlo. *Bitter Victory: The Battle for Sicily, 1943.* New York: Dutton, 1988.

———. *Decision in Normandy.* New York: HarperCollins, 1994.

Divine, Robert A. *The Reluctant Belligerent: American Entry into World War II.* New York: John Wiley, 1965.

Douglas, Roy. *The Advent of War, 1939–40.* New York: St. Martin's Press, 1979.

Dower, John. *War without Mercy: Race and Power in the Pacific War.* New York: Pantheon, 1986.

Eiler, Keith E. *Mobilizing America: Robert P. Patterson and the War Effort, 1940–1945.* Ithaca, N.Y.: Cornell University Press, 1997.

Eisenhower, Dwight D. *Crusade in Europe.* Garden City, N.Y.: Doubleday, 1948. Reprint, Baltimore, Md.: Johns Hopkins University Press, 1997.

Ellis, John. *World War II: A Statistical Survey.* New York: Facts On File, 1993.

Frank, Richard B. *Guadalcanal.* New York: Random House, 1990.

Gaddis, John Lewis. *The United States and the Origins of the Cold War.* New York: Columbia University Press, 1972.

Fussell, Paul. *Wartime: Understanding and Behavior in the Second World War.* New York: Oxford, 1989.

Gilbert, Martin. *The Second World War: A Complete History.* New York: Henry Holt, 1989.

Goodwin, Doris Kearns. *No Ordinary Time: Franklin and Eleanor Roosevelt, The Home Front in World War II.* New York: Simon and Schuster, 1994.

Graham, Dominick, and Shelford Bidwell. *Tug of War: The Battle for Italy, 1943–1945.* New York: St. Martin's Press, 1986.

Hartmann, Susan M. *The Home Front and Beyond: American Women in the 1940s.* Boston, Mass.: Twayne, 1982.

Hastings, Max. *Overlord.* London: Pan Books, 1985.

Hoyt, Edward P. *The GI's War.* New York: McGraw-Hill, 1988.

Irons, Peter. *Justice at War: The Story of the Japanese Internment Cases.* Berkeley: University of California Press, 1983.

Keegan, John. *The Second World War.* New York: Viking, 1989.

———. *Six Armies in Normandy.* New York: Viking, 1982.

Kennedy, David M. *Freedom from Fear: The American People in Depression and War, 1929–1945.* New York: Oxford University Press, 1999.

Kennett, Lee. *GI: The American Soldier in World War II.* New York: Scribner, 1987.

Koppes, Clayton R., and Gregory D. Black. *Hollywood Goes to War.* New York: Free Press, 1987.

Lamb, Richard. *War in Italy.* New York: St. Martin's Press, 1993.

Levine, Alan J. *The Strategic Bombing of Germany, 1940–1945.* Westport, Conn.: Praeger, 1992.

Lewis, Adrian R. *Omaha Beach: A Flawed Victory.* Chapel Hill: University of North Carolina Press, 2001.

Lichtenstein, Nelson. *Labor's War at Home: The CIO in World War II.* New York: Cambridge University Press, 1982.

Lindeman, Gerald F. *The World within War: America's Combat Experience in World War II.* New York: Free Press, 1997.

Linenthal, Edward T., and Tom Engelhardt, eds. *History Wars: The* Enola Gay *and Other Battles for the American Past.* New York: Henry Holt, 1996.

Litoff, Judy Barrett, and David C. Smith, eds. *American Women in a World at War: Contemporary Accounts from World War II.* Wilmington, Del.: Scholarly Resources, 1997.

————. *Since You Went Away: World War II Letters from American Women on the Home Front.* New York: Oxford University Press, 1991.

Lyons, Michael J. *World War II: A Short History.* Englewood Cliffs, N.J.: Prentice Hall, 1989.

McFarland, Stephen L., and Wesley Philips Newton. *To Command the Sky: The Battle for Air Superiority over Germany, 1942–1944.* Washington, D.C.: Smithsonian Institution Press, 1991.

Miller, Nathan. *War at Sea: A Naval History of World War II.* New York: Oxford University Press, 1995.

Miller, Sally M., and Daniel A. Cornford, eds. *American Labor in the Era of World War II.* Westport, Conn.: Praeger, 1995.

Morehouse, Maggi M. *Fighting in the Jim Crow Army: Black Men and Women Remember World War II.* New York: Rowman and Littlefield, 2000.

Moskin, J. Robert. *Mr. Truman's War: The Final Victories of World War II and the Birth of the Postwar World.* New York: Random House, 1996.

Overy, R. J. *Why the Allies Won.* New York: W. W. Norton, 1995.

Parker, Robert Alexander Clarke. *Struggle for Survival: The History of the Second World War.* New York: Oxford University Press, 1989.

Perret, Geoffrey. *Days of Sadness, Years of Triumph: The American People, 1939–1945.* New York: Coward, McCann & Gesghegan, 1973.

————. *There's a War to Be Won: The United States Army in World War II.* New York: Random House, 1991.

Prange, Gordon W. *At Dawn We Slept: The Untold Story of Pearl Harbor.* New York: McGraw-Hill, 1981.

Rhodes, Richard. *The Making of the Atomic Bomb.* New York: Simon and Schuster, 1986.

Schaffer, Ronald. *Wings of Judgment: American Bombing in World War II.* New York: Oxford University Press, 1985.

Schrijvers, Peter. *The Crash of Ruin: American Combat Soldiers in Europe During World War II.* New York: New York University Press, 1998.

Sherry, Michael. *The Rise of American Air Power.* New Haven, Conn.: Yale University Press, 1987.

Sherwin, Martin J. *A World Destroyed: The Atomic Bomb and the Grand Alliance.* New York: Vintage, 1977.

FURTHER READING

Skates, John Ray. *The Invasion of Japan: Alternative to the Bomb.* Columbia: University of South Carolina Press, 1994.

Smith, R. Harris. *OSS: The Secret History of America's First Central Intelligence Agency.* Berkeley: University of California Press, 1972.

Spector, Ronald H. *Eagle Against the Sun: The American War with Japan.* New York: Free Press, 1985.

Takaki, Ronald. *Double Victory: A Multicultural History of America in World War II.* Boston: Little Brown, 2000.

Terkel, Studs. *"The Good War": An Oral History of World War Two.* New York: Pantheon, 1984.

Tuttle, William L. *Daddy's Gone to War: The Second World War in the Lives of America's Children.* New York: Oxford University Press, 1993.

Vatter, Harold G. *The U.S. Economy in World War II.* New York: Columbia University Press, 1985.

Weinberg, Gerhard L. *A World at Arms: A Global History of World War II.* New York: Cambridge University Press, 1994.

Weintraub, Stanley. *The Last Great Victory: The End of World War II, July/August 1945.* New York: Dutton, 1995.

Wilmott, H. P. *The Great Crusade: A New Complete History of the Second World War.* New York: Free Press, 1990.

Wyman, David. *The Abandonment of the Jews: America and the Holocaust, 1941–1945.* New York: Pantheon, 1984.

FICTION

Frank, Anne. *The Diary of a Young Girl.* Garden City, N.Y.: Doubleday, 1952. Reprint, New York: Doubleday, 1995.

Heller, Joseph. *Catch-22.* New York: Simon & Schuster, 1961. Reprint, New York: Scribner, 1996.

Jones, James. *The Thin Red Line.* New York: Scribner, 1962. Reprint, New York: Delta Books, 1998.

Mailer, Norman. *The Naked and the Dead.* New York: Rinehart, 1948. Reprint, New York: Picador USA, 2000.

Shaw, Irwin. *The Young Lions.* New York: Random House, 1948. Reprint, Chicago: University of Chicago Press, 2000.

Vonnegut, Kurt. *Slaughterhouse-Five.* New York: Dell, 1969. Reprint, New York: Dell, 1991.

WEBSITES

Guts and Glory. Available online. URL: http://www.pbs.org/wgbh/amex/guts/index.html. Downloaded on March 27, 2002.

"Powers of Persuasion," The National Archives Exhibition Hall Website. Available online. URL: http://www.nara.gov/exhall/powers/powers.html. Downloaded on March 27, 2002.

United States Holocaust Memorial Museum. Available online. URL: http://www.ushmm.org/education/forstudents/. Downloaded on March 27, 2002.

"Women Come to the Front," The Library of Congress Exhibits Website. Available online. URL: http://lcweb.loc.gov/exhibits/wcf/. Downloaded on March 27, 2002.

Index

Page numbers in *italics* indicate a photograph. Page numbers followed by *m* indicate maps. Page numbers followed by *g* indicate glossary entries. Page numbers in **boldface** indicate box features.